D0375112

PRESENTED
TO:

PRESENTED
BY:

DATE:

GOD'S
DEVOTIONAL
BOOK
FOR WOMEN

HONOR **HB** BOOKS

Inspiration and Motivation for the Seasons of Life

An Imprint of Cook Communications Ministries • Colorado Springs, CO

God's Devotional Book for Women
ISBN 1-56292-571-7

Copyright © 2005 by Honor Books,
An Imprint of Cook Communications Ministries
4050 Lee Vance View
Colorado Springs, CO 80918

Developed by Bordon Books
6532 E. 71st Street, Suite 105
Tulsa, OK 74133

Original manuscript prepared by W.B. Freeman Concepts
Compilation and composition of new elements by The Creative
Word in cooperation with Snapdragon Editorial Group, Inc.
Interior design by LJ Design

GOD'S
DEVOTIONAL
BOOK
FOR WOMEN

INTRODUCTION

The devotionals in this book have been selected to provide a pick-me-up for your day. In the same way a snack or beverage gives you a burst of physical energy, these devotionals are snacks for the soul, awakening you to new insights about yourself and your relationships with family, friends, and colleagues. They will encourage you in your daily walk with God and will serve as a source of motivation as you accomplish your goals and fulfill your dreams.

Our hope is that the material in this book will remind you of God's promise—He is always near. Whether your heart is crying for comfort, protection, an expanded outlook, or direction, through these pages you will see He is both willing and eager to draw you closer to himself, shield you from harm, comfort you with His presence, and encourage you with His Word.

IN GOD YOU CAN TRUST

Dr. Amanda Whitworth was frustrated as she crept up a hill with eight cars in front of her. They were stuck behind a slow-moving truck, and she was in a hurry. Amanda's last patient had needed more attention than was allotted for regular examinations, and she was late leaving to pick up her daughter from day-school. Now she breathed a prayer that she would not be late again. It would be her third time, and because the day-school did not tolerate parental tardiness, she would have to make new arrangements for Allie's afternoon care.

Amanda silently fumed at the truck's progress. No one dared pass the truck on the long hill, as it was impossible to see oncoming cars around it. Suddenly, the truck driver waved his hand indicating that all was clear ahead. As Amanda zipped past him, it occurred to her that this man was probably a stranger to all who passed him—yet nine people trusted their lives and the lives of their families to this man.

What a tremendous picture of how we do all we can do and then must trust even the smallest details of our lives to the care of God, who is a loving Heavenly Father. How comforting to know He can always see exactly what's ahead!

> MY JOB IS TO TAKE CARE OF THE POSSIBLE AND TRUST GOD WITH THE IMPOSSIBLE.
>
> RUTH BELL GRAHAM

THOSE WHO KNOW YOUR NAME WILL TRUST IN YOU, FOR YOU, LORD, HAVE NEVER FORSAKEN THOSE WHO SEEK YOU.

PSALM 9:10 NIV

WISE WORDS

Can anyone think of believing in God without trusting Him? Is it possible to trust in God for the big things like forgiveness and eternal life, and then refuse to trust Him for the little things like clothing and food?

OSWALD C. J. HOFFMANN
LIFE CRUCIFIED, 1959

Blessed are those who trust in the Lord, whose trust is the Lord. They shall be like a tree planted by water, sending out its roots by the stream. It shall not fear when heat comes, and its leaves shall stay green; in the year of drought it is not anxious, and it does not cease to bear fruit.
    JEREMIAH 17:7-8 NRSV

GOD LOVES GOOD NEIGHBORS

"I OFTEN HAVE THOUGHT that we are a little old-fashioned here in the Ozark hills," writes Laura Ingalls Wilder in *Little House in the Ozarks.* "Now I know we are, because we had a 'working' in our neighborhood this winter. That is a blessed, old-fashioned way of helping out a neighbor.

"While the winter was warm, still it has been much too cold to be without firewood; and this neighbor, badly crippled with rheumatism, was not able to get up his winter's wood. . . . So the men of the neighborhood gathered together one morning and dropped in on him. With cross-cut saws and axes, they took possession of his wood lot. . . . By night there was enough wood ready . . . to last the rest of the winter.

"The women did their part, too. All morning they kept arriving with well-filled baskets, and at noon a long table was filled with a country neighborhood dinner. . . . When the dishes were washed, they sewed, knit, crocheted, and talked for the rest of the afternoon. It was a regular old-fashioned good time, and we all went home with the feeling expressed by a newcomer when he said, 'Don't you know I'm proud to live in a neighborhood like this where they turn out and help one another when it's needed.'"[1]

> **Kindness** is a language that the deaf can hear and the blind can see. MARK TWAIN

Great is his **love** toward us,
and the **faithfulness** of the LORD
endures **forever.**

PSALM 117:2 NIV

new insights into ageless questions

Q I know I'm commanded to love my neighbor as myself, but it's pretty hard to do when I don't know my neighbors—and never even see them! How can I begin to take more seriously Jesus' command to love my neighbors?

First of all, Jesus meant that we are to love all people we encounter, not literally just our neighbors. Still, loving our physical neighbors is a great place to start. Consider tying an invitation to the door of each person on your street introducing yourself and suggesting a pot-luck block party. Include your phone number, and ask interested persons to give you a call. You may find out that other people want to meet their neighbors too. And once you know them, it will be easier to find ways to show them Jesus' love.

What if I extend love to my neighbor, but it isn't returned?

God reached out to us in love through His Son, Jesus Christ. Through the centuries, many millions have turned their backs on Him, but His love continues to shine brightly in our world. Not everyone will return your gift of love, but some will—and that's the point.

MAKE YOUR MOTTO MATTER

You may bring to your office, and put in a frame,
a motto as fine as its paint,
but if you're a crook when you're playing the game,
that motto won't make you a saint.
You can stick up the placards all over the wall,
but here is a word I announce:
It is not the motto that hangs on the wall,
but the motto you live, that counts.
If the motto says, "Smile,"
and you carry a frown:
"Do it now," and you linger and wait;
if the motto says "Help,"
and you trample men down;
if the motto says, "Love," and you hate—
you won't get away with the mottoes you stall,
for truth will come forth with a bounce.
It is not the motto that hangs on the wall,
but the motto you live, that counts.[2]

> **The tree** is known and recognized and judged by its fruit.
> MATTHEW 12:33 AMP

People may **doubt** what you **say**,
but they will always **believe**
what you **do**.

The motto on the side of a fresh fish delivery truck reads, "If it swims, we have it!" Wouldn't it be great if you had such a clearly stated motto describing your purpose as a believer in Jesus Christ? Perhaps it would help you stay focused on Him and His eternal work. Consider making one of the following mottoes your own, or write one yourself!

- "Christians aren't perfect, just forgiven."
- "My boss is a Jewish carpenter."
- "Jesus is my best friend."
- "Be patient. God's not finished with me yet."
- "God answers prayers 24-7."
- "Real women love Jesus."

"God has a HISTORY of using the insignificant to accomplish the IMPOSSIBLE.

RICHARD EXLEY

ALL THINGS CAN BE USEFUL FOR GOD

In order to communicate among themselves, Serbian shepherd boys developed an ingenious system. They would stick the blades of their long knives into the ground of a pasture, and when one of the boys sensed an approaching cattle thief, he would strike the handle of his knife sharply. The vibration created a signal that could be picked up by other shepherd boys, their ears pressed tightly against the ground. It was by this unique system that they outwitted thieves who tried to creep up on their flocks and herds under the cover of darkness and tall corn.

Most of the shepherd boys grew up and forgot about their ground signals, but one boy remembered. Twenty-five years after he left the pastures, he made one of the greatest inventions of the modern era. Michael Pupin changed the telephone from a device used only to speak across a city to a long-distance instrument that could be heard across a continent.

Something you take for granted today, something others may consider to be insignificant or ordinary, may actually become your key to greatness. Look around you. What is it that God has put at your disposal?

Who's Who:

Moses

In Exodus, chapter 4, Moses is involved in a discussion with God regarding his suitability to represent the Israelites. "What if they do not believe me or listen to me?" he asks God. "What is that in your hand?" the Lord replies. "A staff," Moses says. Then God tells Moses to throw the staff on the ground, and when he does, it immediately becomes a serpent. God gave Moses the ability to use whatever was in his hand at the moment to demonstrate not Moses' power, but God's power!

What's in your hand? Is it a wooden spoon? Bake cookies to take to a neighbor or a shut-in. Is it a steering wheel? Volunteer to drive an extra carpool or take an elderly person to the doctor. Whatever is in your hand, God can use it for His glory.

KEEP FAMILY LOVE GROWING

"THE FAMILY," says Mother Teresa, "is the place to learn Jesus. God has sent the family—together as husband and wife and children—to be His love."

In *Words to Love By,* Mother Teresa writes, "Once a lady came to me in great sorrow and told me that her daughter had lost her husband and a child. All the daughter's hatreds had turned on the mother. She wouldn't even see the mother.

"So I said, 'Now you think a bit about the little things that your daughter liked when she was a child. Maybe flowers or a special food. Try to give her some of these things without looking

> WHEN **MOTHER TERESA** RECEIVED HER **NOBEL PRIZE** SHE WAS ASKED, "WHAT CAN WE DO TO PROMOTE **WORLD PEACE?**" SHE REPLIED, "GO HOME AND **LOVE** YOUR **FAMILY.**"
>
> MOTHER TERESA

for a return.'

"And she started doing some of these things, like putting the daughter's favorite flower on the table, or leaving a beautiful piece of cloth for her. And she did not look for a return from the daughter.

"Several days later the daughter said, 'Mommy, come. I love you. I want you.'

"It was very beautiful.

"By being reminded of the joy of childhood, the daughter reconnected with her family life. She must have had a happy childhood to go back to the joy and happiness of her mother's love."[3]

Let love and faithfulness never leave you;
bind them around your neck,
write them on the tablet of your heart.

PROVERBS 3:3 NIV

TOP 10 TIPS for Showing Your Family How Much You Love Them

1. START EACH DAY WITH A COMPLIMENT FOR EACH FAMILY MEMBER.

2. LEAVE LOVING NOTES IN PLACES LIKE BACKPACKS AND BRIEFCASES.

3. ONCE A MONTH, HAVE A "DATE" WITH EACH CHILD.

4. OFFER TO DO SOMEONE ELSE'S CHORES.

5. MAKE MEALTIMES SPECIAL TOGETHER-TIMES.

6. PRAISE EVEN THE SMALLEST ACCOMPLISHMENTS.

7. WATCH A FAVORITE VIDEO— FOR THE HUNDREDTH TIME!

8. ASK HOW EACH CHILD'S DAY WAS, THEN REALLY LISTEN TO THE ANSWER.

9. PROVIDE AN ENDLESS SUPPLY OF HUGS.

10. PRAY TOGETHER BEFORE BEDTIME.

CONSIDER THIS!

A popular sentiment often seen painted on plaques at craft fairs or embroidered on T-shirts reads: "Lord, please put Your arm around my shoulders and Your hand over my mouth." Those words may make us smile, but they are also wise words as they speak to the problem we all have of saying things that we really wish we hadn't—things that do not edify others and do not bring glory to God.

Making cutting, sarcastic comments can become a habit that's hard to break. Ask God to put His hand over your mouth so that you might stop and think before saying an unkind thing.

Cold words freeze people, and hot words scorch them, and bitter words make them bitter, and wrathful words make them wrathful. Kind words also produce their image on men's souls; and a beautiful image it is. They smooth, and quiet, and comfort the hearer.

BLAISE PASCAL

THE POWER OF WORDS

Birds sing and never have to apologize for their songs.

Dogs bark and kittens meow and never have to say, "I'm sorry for what I just said."

Lions roar and hyenas howl, but they never have to retract their statements as being untrue.

The fact is, the members of the animal kingdom are themselves, and they are true in their expression to what they were created to be.

Many times we human beings find ourselves embarrassed at our own words—feeling apologetic, caught in an awkward moment, or recognizing we have spoken the wrong words at

PEOPLE WITH TACT HAVE LESS TO RETRACT.

the wrong time—because we have begun evaluating the performance of others and have developed a critical attitude.

The bluejay doesn't criticize the robin. The kitten doesn't make snide remarks about the puppy. The lion doesn't ridicule the hyena. In like manner, we should not put down others whom we can never fully understand, never fully appreciate, or never fully emulate.

Stick to singing your own song today, and appreciate the uniqueness of those around you. You will easily avoid putting your foot in your mouth!

The **heart** of the righteous **weighs** its **answers,** but the **mouth** of the **wicked** gushes **evil.**

PROVERBS 15:28 NIV

JUST DO IT

Two sisters had held a desire from childhood to, one day, go to the mission field together. As they approached midlife, they realized they were both well established in their professions, and they began to investigate where they might go to serve God. After several months of talking to various missionary agencies, one of the sisters quit her job and moved to South America, where she became involved in pioneering churches.

The other sister, however, decided the hazards of the mission field were too great. She would remain at home and make even more money. "I'll go later," she said as she bid her sister good-bye. Two years later she died in an accident on the job. She had "saved" her life, only to lose it.

Safety is an illusion apart from God. Many people trust in their jobs—unaware that their companies are on the brink of bankruptcy. Others trust in the government—unaware that funds are diminishing and laws are subject to change. Still others trust in their own abilities, never counting on accidents or illness.

If the Lord has spoken to your heart to "Go," be swift to respond when He opens the door for you to do so.

> I HAVE HELD MANY THINGS IN MY HANDS AND LOST THEM ALL; BUT THE THINGS I HAVE PLACED IN GOD'S HANDS, THOSE I ALWAYS POSSESS.
>
> JOYCE EARLINE STEELBURG

I KNOW WHOM I HAVE BELIEVED, AND AM PERSUADED THAT HE IS ABLE TO KEEP THAT WHICH I HAVE COMMITTED UNTO HIM AGAINST THAT DAY.

2 TIMOTHY 1:12 KJV

WISE WORDS

In *Discipleship Journal* author Elaine Creasman writes:

"Pursuit of 'good things' can hinder obedience. It has been said that 'the good is the enemy of the best.' I think of times my husband has asked me to do one thing for him during the day. When he gets home from work, I tell him all the good things I have done. But the question he always has for me is, 'What about the thing I asked you to do?'

"Many times I have answered, 'I forgot,' or 'I didn't have time.' Or I've dismissed his request as trivial.

"God asks that same question of us: 'What about the thing I asked you to do?'

"I'm sure Abraham could have thought of a lot of good things to do instead of taking Isaac to be sacrificed. But I see no excuses in Genesis 22. God commanded; Abraham obeyed."

Trivia

Fun

There are many verses in the Bible that promise God's help when we are in trouble. See if you can match the Scripture with the Scripture reference.

We say with confidence, "The Lord is my helper; I will not be afraid."
- A. Psalm 46:1
- B. Hebrews 13:6
- C. Psalm 68:19

God is our refuge and strength, an ever-present help in trouble.
- A. Isaiah 59:1
- B. Psalm 28:7
- C. Psalm 46:1

The Lord is my strength and my shield; my heart trusts in him, and I am helped.
- A. Psalm 68:19
- B. Hebrews 13:6
- C. Psalm 28:7

Surely the arm of the Lord is not too short to save, nor his ear too dull to hear.
- A. Psalm 72:12
- B. Isaiah 59:1
- C. Psalm 46:1

It is the Sovereign Lord who helps me.
- A. Isaiah 50:9
- B. Hebrews 2:18
- C. Psalm 72:12

Answers found in *The Holy Bible. Directly quoted from the* NIV.

LET GO AND LET GOD

When I **come** to the
end of my rope, **God** is
there to take over.

The end of our human abilities is our opportunity to turn to God. But giving up our independence to depend on God isn't necessarily easy. We are often like the woman in this story reported in the Los Angeles Times:

A screaming woman, trapped in a car dangling from a freeway transition road in East Los Angeles, was rescued Saturday morning. . . . A half dozen passing motorists stopped, grabbed some ropes from out of their vehicles, tied the ropes to the back of the woman's car, and hung on until the fire units arrived. A ladder was extended from below to help stabilize the car while firefighters tied the vehicle to tow trucks with cable and chains.

"Every time we would move the car," said one rescuer, "she'd yell and scream. She was in pain."

It took almost two and a half hours for the passersby, CHP officers, tow truck drivers, and firefighters—about twenty-five people in all—to secure the car and pull the woman to safety.

"It was kinda funny," L.A. County Fire Captain Ross Marshall recalled later. "She kept saying, 'I'll do it myself.'"[4]

God has said, "Never
will I leave you;
Never will I forsake you."

HEBREWS 13:5 NIV

CAST YOUR WORRIES ON HIM

PEOPLE WHO CONTINUALLY worry about every detail of their lives are like a patient in a mental hospital who stood with her ear pressed against the wall.

"What are you doing?" an attendant asked with curiosity.

"Shhhh," the woman whispered, beckoning to the attendant to join her at the wall.

The attendant pressed her ear to the wall and stood there for several moments listening intently. "I can't hear anything," she said.

"No," the patient replied with a furrowed brow. "It's been like that all day!"

Some worry about what might be said. Others worry about what hasn't been said. Some worry about what might happen. Others worry about what hasn't happened which should have happened by now. Some worry about their futures, while others fret over the consequences of their past.

We were created to live abundant lives in our minds, our bodies, and our spirits. Like a flower we were meant to blossom, not to wither on the vine. Put Jesus in charge of your worries today and walk in newness of life!

> **Worry is** like a rocking chair: It gives you something to do, but doesn't get you anywhere.

Casting the whole of your care [all your anxieties, all your worries, all your concerns, once and for all] on Him; for He cares for you affectionately, and cares about you watchfully.

1 PETER 5:7 AMP

It seems the harder I try not to worry, the more I do! How can I conquer the worry habit?

To overcome the temptation to worry, we can take a cue from—believe it or not—extreme snow skiers who love to ski through groves of trees. It sounds crazy, but they love skiing on fresh, untouched snow, even if it means taking the risk of running into a tree. In an article in *Outside* magazine, writer Tim Etchells provides the key: "Even more so than in deep snow or moguls, what you focus your eyes on becomes critical in the woods. Look at the spaces between the trees—the exits where you hope to be traveling. Don't stare at what you don't want to hit." Likewise, to avoid worrying about the obstacles in life that you encounter, just shift your focus from the "trees" to God!

ENCOURAGE ONE ANOTHER

In *Especially for a Woman*[5], Ann Kiemel Anderson writes in her unique style about her sister: "Jan taught 3rd grade once, a long time ago. One bright-eyed boy would stand at her desk, watch her, and talk to her, all the while wrapping his finger around a piece of her hair into a little curl. He thought Jan was the shining star in the night. Over and over, however, he did poorly in his work assignments and daily quizzes.

> **Congenial conversation —what a pleasure! The right word at the right time— beautiful!**
>
> PROVERBS 15:23 MSG

"One day Jan stopped, looked at him, and said, 'Rodney, you are very smart. You could be doing so well in school. In fact, you are one of my finest students . . . ' Before she could continue to tell him that he should be doing much better in school . . . he looked up at her with sober, large eyes:

"'I did not know that!'

"From that moment on, Rodney began to change. His papers were neater, cleaner, and his spelling improved. He was one of her top students—all because she affirmed him. She told him something no one ever had before, and it changed his life."

Nobody ever became ill or died from receiving too much genuine praise and encouragement. But who can count the wounded hearts, weary souls, and troubled minds that have resulted from their lack!

We should seize every opportunity
to give encouragement.
Encouragement is oxygen to the soul.

GEORGE M. ADAMS

to do | urgent

Make a list of five people you know who are in special need of encouragement this week. This might be:

- A friend starting a new job
- Your child's teacher
- A member of your church who is dealing with a family crisis

Send a card or write a note of cheer to each one. In each note, also mention something that you particularly admire about the recipient.

Lord, thank You for the privilege of offering a word of encouragement to the people listed below. I know they are precious to You:

1. _____
2. _____
3. _____
4. _____
5. _____

booklist

read more about it...prayer

- *What Happens When Women Pray*
  by Evelyn Christenson

- *What Happens When God Answers Prayer*
  by Evelyn Christenson

- *Prayers of a Godly Woman*
  by Jim Gallery

- *Handle with Prayer*
  by Charles Stanley

- *Praying God's Word*
  by Beth Moore

- *Becoming a Woman of Prayer*
  by Cynthia Heald

- *Power of a Praying Woman*
  by Stormie Omartian

THE POWER OF PRAYER

WHY PRAY?

We pray because prayer opens up the floodgates of God's infinite grace and power to flow toward the person in need. God can act without prayer, but He chooses to operate within the boundaries of human will and invitation. He allows us to participate in His work on earth with each prayer.

Leonard Ravenhill once said about prayer, "One might estimate the weight of the world, tell the size of the celestial city, count the stars of heaven, measure the speed of lightning, and tell the time of the rising and the setting of the sun—but you cannot estimate prayer power. Prayer is as vast as God because He is behind it. Prayer is as mighty as God because He has committed himself to answer it."

A sign in a cotton factory read: "If your threads get tangled, send for the foreman." One day a new worker got her threads tangled. The more she tried to disentangle them, the worse the situation grew. Finally, she sent for the foreman. He asked, "Why didn't you send for me earlier?" She replied, "I was doing my best." He answered, "No, your best would have been to send for me."

When we face a tough situation, our first response should be to ask for God's help. He longs to be our helper and to be fully involved in our lives.

> **Give your** troubles to God: He will be up all night anyway.

He will **not** allow your foot to slip;

He who **keeps** you will not **slumber.**

PSALM 121:3 NASB

"You are never so **HIGH** as when you are on your knees."

JEAN HODGES

PRAY, PRAY, PRAY

On a stormy day, with two experienced guides, a woman climbed the Weisshorn in the Swiss Alps. As they neared the peak, the woman—exhilarated by the view before her—sprang forward and was almost blown away by a gust of wind. One of the guides caught her and pulled her down, saying, "On your knees, madam! You are safe here only on your knees."

We typically regard "on our knees" as the standard position for prayer, but talking to God isn't limited to any position. He can hear us, regardless.

Three Christian women were talking once about the "best" positions for prayer. One argued the importance of holding one's hands together and pointing them upward. The second advocated that prayer was best when one was stretched out on the floor. The third thought standing was better than kneeling. As they talked, a telephone repairman listened as he worked on a nearby phone system.

Finally, he could contain himself no longer and interjected, "I have found that the most powerful prayer I ever made was while I was dangling upside down from a power pole, suspended forty feet above the ground."

The important thing is not your position of prayer, but the fact that you do pray!

Who's Who:

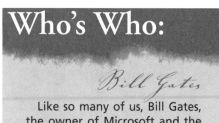

Like so many of us, Bill Gates, the owner of Microsoft and the richest man in the world, has an e-mail address. When The *New Yorker* magazine published that address, Gates woke one morning to find five thousand new messages in his inbox! He was overwhelmed and had to install filtering programs so that in the future, only important e-mail messages would get through.

Unlike Bill Gates, God is never overwhelmed by too many "messages." There are no filters on God's inbox, and He considers each message important and worthy of His attention. In fact, God wants to hear from His children—the more the better!

BEING THERE

UNTIL THE TIME JANE learned she needed an operation, the question "Who will take care of me if I get sick?" had only been hypothetical. As a single woman, she hadn't given much thought to how she would survive a major illness or operation. As it turned out, she found that she had a "loving menagerie of friends" who "cobbled together a schedule of ministry and then passed the baton from one to the next while I marveled at my good fortune."[6]

Stephanie was the ringmaster, the one by her side at the hospital, who also helped her check her incision and take showers. Bob drove up from Los Angeles with his dog to stay for a few days after she returned home. Peggy brought over Thai take-out food. Ann arrived with a bread machine and bags of groceries. She also made soup, mopped the kitchen floor, and did the laundry. Michelle brought mail from the office and drove her to doctors' appointments.

It was amazing to Jane that these various people hardly knew each other when they first began helping her, but by the time she recovered, they had all become friends. Being a servant has wonderful rewards. Many times in our serving we receive much more than we ever gave away.

lighten up

We Need Each Other

A young woman was waiting for a bus in a dangerous part of town one evening. A rookie policeman approached her and asked, "Want me to wait with you?"

She replied, "Thank you, but that's not necessary. I'm not afraid."

"Well, then," he said, grinning, "would you mind waiting with me?"

"God didn't **save** you to be a **sensation**. He **saved** you to be a **servant.**"

prepares you for honors. PROVERBS 29:23 MSG

SOWING SEEDS OF KINDNESS

Joy Sprague knows how to brighten the days of her customers. As the postmaster for Little Cranberry Island, Maine, she actually has customers competing to get their pictures on her post-office wall. Every twenty-fifth customer to use the U.S. Postal Service's Express Mail has a "mug shot" taken and hung on the wall of the post office—which is actually a portion of the general store—and then is given a plate of Joy's home-baked cream puffs!

That's not all Joy does to make Little Cranberry, population ninety, a friendlier place. She operates a mail-order stamp business that is so popular her tiny post office ranks fourth in sales out of 450 outlets in Maine.

> A GOOD DEED IS NEVER LOST; HE WHO SOWS COURTESY REAPS FRIENDSHIP, AND HE WHO PLANTS KINDNESS GATHERS LOVE.
>
> SAINT BASIL

Why? Most of Joy's customers are summer visitors who want to stay in contact with the island. Joy sends a snapshot of an island scene and a handwritten note about island events along with each order.

One of the residents has said, "She invents ways to bring pleasure to others." Joy has received praise from the U.S. Postmaster General and has the warm affection not only of the local residents, but of friends across America who delight in corresponding with her.

Why not ask the Lord to give you creative ideas that will brighten others' lives today. Perhaps a brief telephone call or post card will remind them how important they really are to you and to God, their Heavenly Father.

> WHENEVER WE HAVE AN OPPORTUNITY, LET US WORK FOR THE GOOD OF ALL, AND ESPECIALLY THOSE OF THE FAMILY OF FAITH.
>
> GALATIANS 6:10 NRSV

WISE WORDS

Christ has no body now on earth but yours. Yours are the only hands with which He can do His work, yours are the only feet with which He can go about the world, yours are the only eyes through which His compassion can shine forth upon a troubled world. Christ has no body now on earth but yours.

TERESA OF AVILA

MAKING CHRIST YOUR PARTNER

> I MAKE IT A **RULE** OF CHRISTIAN DUTY **NEVER** TO GO TO A PLACE WHERE THERE IS **NOT ROOM** FOR MY **MASTER** AS WELL AS MYSELF.
>
> JOHN NEWTON

AN ATTRACTIVE single woman had a job that required her to travel a great deal. When a new female colleague was added to her department, she told her how happy she was to have another woman on the team. She related how she often felt isolated when she found herself the only woman at breakfast in a hotel restaurant, or one of only a handful of women on a commuter flight.

"Do the men ever bother you?" the new young colleague asked.

"Rarely," the woman replied.

"Wow," said the young colleague. "You are so beautiful, I would think you are approached a great deal by men you really don't care to meet."

"No," the woman explained, "I just say five words, and immediately I am left alone."

"Five words?" the young colleague asked, hoping to gain a valuable tip. "What are they?"

"When I am approached by a man," the woman said, "I simply ask, 'Are you a born-again Christian?' "

"Has anyone ever said 'yes'?" the younger asked.

"Rarely," said the woman. "And when such men want to talk to me anyway, I always have an enjoyable conversation, because Jesus can be part of it."

Don't be **teamed** with those who do **not love** the Lord.... How can a Christian be a **partner** with one who doesn't **believe?**

2 CORINTHIANS 6:14,15 TLB

TOP 10 TIPS

for Keeping Christ
in the Workplace

1. BEGIN YOUR DAY WITH PRAYER, ASKING GOD
   TO BE A PART OF EVERY DECISION YOU MAKE.

2. KEEP A FAVORITE DEVOTIONAL OR INSPIRATIONAL
   BOOK IN YOUR DESK TO READ DURING BREAKS.

3. PUT PEOPLE FIRST WHEN YOU SCHEDULE YOUR DAY.

4. IF YOU'RE ALLOWED TO LISTEN TO MUSIC DURING
   THE DAY, TUNE IN TO A CHRISTIAN STATION.

5. BEFORE MAKING DIFFICULT DECISIONS,
   THINK OF BIBLICAL PRINCIPLES THAT APPLY.

6. DON'T TAKE CREDIT FOR SOMETHING SOMEONE ELSE DOES.

7. WHEN YOU'RE WRONG, ADMIT
   IT AND ASK FOR FORGIVENESS.

8. GREET THOSE YOU ENCOUNTER WITH A CHEERFUL SMILE.

9. RESPECT THE AUTHORITY IN YOUR WORKPLACE, WHILE
   REMEMBERING GOD IS THE ULTIMATE AUTHORITY IN YOUR LIFE.

10. ALWAYS DO YOUR BEST, AS A WAY OF HONORING CHRIST.

THE DIFFERENCE
A SMILE MAKES

The practice of one particular church was to dismiss the children in the Sunday morning service just prior to the sermon. The children would all march forward in a make-shift processional and sing a song as they passed the pulpit on their way to hear a sermon prepared just for them. The pastor enjoyed this part of the service. He made it a point to smile at each child and to receive a smile in return.

> **A happy** heart makes the face cheerful.
>
> PROVERBS 15:13 NIV

To his surprise, one morning a curly-haired four-year-old girl ran out of the procession and threw herself into her mother's arms, sobbing deeply. The pastor sought out the mother after the service to see what had happened. The child had told her, "I smiled at God, but He didn't smile back."

The pastor's heart sank. He had failed to smile, and the child's joy had turned to torment.

We may think our smiles do not represent God to another person, but they just might! Genuine smiles are a sign of affirmation, appreciation, and love.

Your smile can bring hope and change the countenance of someone today. Give it a try.

What sunshine is to flowers, smiles are to humanity. They are but trifles, to be sure, but, scattered along life's pathway, the good they do is inconceivable.

JOSEPH ADDISON

#1   Smiles come in many shapes and sizes. They also come in the form of encouraging cards and letters to children struggling with life-threatening illnesses.

#2   The Make a Child Smile organization was created by a young woman named Alexandra, originally from Brazil. In 1998, someone sent her a link to the Web site of a nine-year-old girl who was battling cancer. Alex responded to the re-

#3 quest of the girl's parents to send her cards to cheer her up. The idea so intrigued her that she created another Web site to bring smiles to the faces of other sick children.

#4   Check out the site at http://www.makeachildsmile.org/ and find out how you can make a child smile!

#5

#6

#7

#8

#9

#10

CONSIDER THIS!

A Morning Prayer

So far, the day is going great, Lord! I haven't gossiped, I haven't lost my temper, and I haven't been selfish or grouchy. But in a few minutes, I'm going to actually get out of bed, and for the rest of the day I'm going to need Your help!

It's true. Temptation begins the minute we open our eyes each day and doesn't let up until we close them at night. That's why it's so important to begin every day with a prayer for strength to overcome whatever temptation may come our way throughout our waking hours.

AVOIDING TEMPTATION

As a teen, Megan arrived home from school just in time to watch an hour of "soap operas" before doing her homework. She enjoyed the escape into the TV world and wasn't really aware that the programs were creating an inordinate amount of sexual curiosity in her. Over months and even years of watching her two "soaps," Megan's perspective on life took a shift. She began to think, *Relationships don't need to be pure—in fact, the impure ones seem more exciting. Fidelity doesn't matter, as long as a person is happy.*

As a college student, Megan found it easy to participate in "one-night stands." Then, after a short marriage ended in catastrophe as a result of her infidelity, she sought help from a counselor. At the outset, it was difficult for the counselor to understand why Megan had engaged in extramarital affairs. She had been a model teenager at home, church, and school as far as her public behavior was concerned. Finally, the counselor discovered the source of the temptations that drove Megan to participate in her supposed hidden life.

What we see on TV inevitably becomes a part of our memory bank, becoming background information for "justified" behavior. If what you see isn't what you want to do, then change what you see.

> **WATCH OUT FOR TEMPTATION— THE MORE YOU SEE OF IT THE BETTER IT LOOKS.**

"Keep watching and praying, that you may not come into temptation."

MARK 14:38 NASB

Be kind to one another,
TENDERHEARTED,
forgiving one another,
as God in CHRIST has forgiven you.

EPHESIANS 4:32 NRSV

FORGIVE AND FORGET

A man once had too much to drink at a party. First, he made a foolish spectacle of himself—even to the point of wearing the proverbial lampshade as a hat—and then he passed out. Friends helped his wife take him home and put him to bed. The next morning he was very remorseful and asked his wife to forgive him. She agreed to "forgive and forget" the incident.

As the months went by, however, the wife referred to the incident from time to time, always with a little note of ridicule and shame in her voice. Finally, the man grew weary of being reminded of his bad behavior and said, "I thought you were going to forgive and forget."

"I have forgiven and forgotten," the wife argued, "but I just don't want you to forget that I have forgiven and forgotten."

Once we have confronted an offender, we must remember nothing is gained from harboring unforgiveness in our hearts. Forgiveness requires a healing process inside us—to the point where we no longer feel any pain at the memory of what the other person did or said to injure us.

We "forget" when we no longer hurt! When you make a commitment to forgive another person, ask the Lord to heal you of the impact of that person's behavior on your life. Forgive, forget, and start living again.

Who's Who:

Ronald Reagan

President Ronald Reagan's attitude of forgiveness after the attempt on his life in 1982 made a great impression on his daughter, Patti Davis. Later, she wrote in her book *Angels Don't Die*, "I give endless prayers of thanks to whatever angels circled my father, because a Devastator bullet, which miraculously had not exploded, was found a quarter inch from his heart.

"The following day my father said he knew his physical healing was directly dependent on his ability to forgive John Hinckley. By showing me that forgiveness is the key to everything, including physical health and healing, he gave me an example of Christ-like thinking."

HOW Do YOU MEASURE Up?

Each year Americans give billions of dollars to charitable causes. In fact, annual giving in the U.S. is more than the gross domestic product of many of the world's countries! But Jesus gives us a different picture of generosity in Mark 12:41-44. This brief passage describes Jesus in the temple, observing rich person after rich person passing by the offering box and putting in great amounts of money. Then, when a poor old woman passes by and drops in two small coins, Jesus ignores the rich and their big gifts to praise the woman and her small gift.

Why? As He says, "They all gave out of their wealth; but she, out of her poverty, put in everything—all she had to live on." In other words, it's not the size of the gift that matters to God—it's the size of the sacrifice.

How Generous Are You?

A) I think the poor just aren't trying. If they worked harder, they wouldn't need handouts!

B) I think the government should take care of the poor.

C) I try to give whenever I see someone in desperate need.

D) I give regularly, and I'm always asking God to show me

THE BLESSED ACT OF GIVING

YOU MAY GIVE WITHOUT LOVING, BUT YOU CANNOT LOVE WITHOUT GIVING.

Most authorities believe King David's Temple was built on Mount Moriah where Abraham was told to sacrifice Isaac. But there's another Hebrew legend that presents a different story.

The legend says that two brothers lived on adjoining farms which were divided from the peak to the base of the mountain. The younger brother lived alone, unmarried. The older brother had a large family.

One night during grain harvest, the older brother awoke and thought, *My brother is all alone. To cheer his heart, I will take some of my sheaves and lay them on his side of the field.*

At the same hour, the younger brother awoke and thought, *My brother has a large family and greater needs than I do. As he sleeps, I'll put some of my sheaves on his side of the field.* Each brother went out carrying sheaves to the other's field and met halfway. When they declared their intentions to each other, they dropped their sheaves and embraced. It is at that place, the legend claims, the Temple was built.

Whether this story is true or not, it exemplifies the best expression of love—giving. Giving is one of life's best relation-builders.

Jesus said, "God so loved the world that he gave his only Son, so that everyone who believes in him may not perish but may have eternal life."

JOHN 3:16 NRSV

EVEN DEATH CAN'T SEPARATE US

Tom Dooley was a young doctor who gave up an easy career to organize hospitals and pour out his life in service to afflicted people in Southeast Asia. As he lay dying of cancer at age thirty-four, Dooley wrote to the president of Notre Dame, his alma mater:

> BEING AT PEACE WITH YOURSELF IS A DIRECT RESULT OF FINDING PEACE WITH GOD.
>
> OLIN MILLER

"Dear Father Hesburgh: They've got me down. Flat on the back, with plaster, sandbags, and hot water bottles. I've contrived a way of pumping the bed up a bit so that, with a long reach, I can get to my typewriter . . . Two things prompt this note to you. The first is that whenever my cancer acts up a bit . . . I turn inward. Less do I think of my hospitals around the world, or of ninety-four doctors, fund-raisers, and the like. More do I think of one Divine Doctor and my personal fund of grace . . . I have monstrous phantoms; all men do. And inside and outside the wind blows. But when the time comes, like now, then the storm around me does not matter. The winds within me do not matter. Nothing human or earthly can touch me. A peace gathers in my heart. What seems unpossessable, I can possess. What seems unfathomable, I can fathom. What is unutterable, I can utter. Because I can pray. I can communicate. How do people endure anything on earth if they cannot have God?"[7]

THE PEACE OF GOD, WHICH PASSETH ALL UNDERSTANDING, SHALL KEEP YOUR HEARTS AND MINDS THROUGH CHRIST JESUS.

PHILIPPIANS 4:7 KJV

WISE WORDS

We picture death as coming to destroy; let us rather picture Christ as coming to save. We think of death as ending; let us rather think of life as beginning, and that more abundantly. We think of losing; let us think of gaining. We think of parting, let us think of meeting. We think of going away; let us think of arriving. And as the voice of death whispers "You must go from earth," let us hear the voice of Christ saying, "You are but coming to Me!"

NORMAN MACLEOD

Have you ever noticed that a tightly woven braid looks like it is made from only two strands of hair? But despite appearances, it's impossible to make a braid from only two strands. If two strands are entwined, they will easily unravel. In fact, what looks like only two requires a third. Though not evident to the eye, the third strand keeps the braid together. Likewise in a Christian marriage, God serves as the third strand, keeping the other two—the husband and the wife—together.

LOVE FOR A LIFETIME

Nothing beats **love**
at **first sight**
except **love** with **insight.**

Two lifelong friends in their early fifties began to argue over the forthcoming marriage of one of them to a man who was only in his thirties.

"I just don't believe in May-December marriages," the friend said. "After all, December is going to find in May the strength and virility of springtime, but whatever is May going to find in December?"

The bride-to-be thought for a moment and then replied with a twinkle in her eye, "Christmas."

Many couples who claim they "fell in love at first sight" look back after years of marriage and adjust their opinions, saying, "I was infatuated," or "We felt an immediate attraction," or "There was electricity between us when we first met." Love, however, is a word they have come to cherish—it is something they now share that is far richer and meaningful than the emotions they felt "at first sight."

One of the great qualities about genuine love is that it grows and deepens over time. Time is life's nursery for love. Tend to it as you would your most cherished plant, and love's fragrance will continually remain.

The **beginning** of wisdom
is this: Get **wisdom**
and whatever else you get,
get **insight.**

PROVERBS 4:7 NRSV

TURN WHINING INTO THANKSGIVING

JESUS CAN TURN WATER INTO WINE, BUT HE CAN'T TURN YOUR WHINING INTO ANYTHING.

MARK STEELE

Rather than whining that we don't have certain things in our lives or that something is wrong, we need to take positive action. Here are four steps toward turning whining into thanksgiving.

1. Give something away. When you give something, you create both a physical and a mental space for something new and better to come into your life. Although you may think you are "lacking" something in life, when you give you demonstrate you have abundance to spare.

2. Narrow your goals. Don't expect everything good to come into your life all at once. When you focus your expectations toward specific and reachable goals, you are more apt to direct your time and energy toward reaching them.

3. Change your vocabulary from "I need" to "I want." Most of the things we think we need are actually things we want. When you receive them, you are more likely to be thankful for them as luxuries rather than necessities.

4. Thanksgiving is a choice we make, shoose to be thankful for what you already have. Every one of us has more things to be thankful for than we could begin to recount in a day.

Do everything **without** complaining or **arguing**, so that you may become blameless and **pure**, children of God without fault.

PHILIPPIANS 2:14-15 NIV

| new insights into ageless questions

I recently decided to forgive a person who had wronged me. Although I feel in my heart that I've forgiven her, I just can't forget the wrong itself! The incident keeps re-playing over and over in my mind. How can I forget as well as forgive?

In an article in *Guideposts,* Holocaust survivor and renowned Christian writer Corrie ten Boom wrote that she once was having the same problem. When she asked God for help, it came in the form of a Lutheran pastor, who presented the following illustration, a beautiful answer to this question that everyone encounters sooner or later:

"Up in that church tower," he said, nodding out the window, "is a bell which is rung by pulling on a rope. But you know what? After the sexton lets go of the rope the bell keeps on swinging. First 'ding,' then 'dong.' Slower and slower until there's a final dong and it stops. I believe the same thing is true of forgiveness. When we forgive, we take our hand off the rope. But if we've been tugging at our grievances for a long time, we mustn't be surprised if the old angry thoughts keep coming for a while. They're just the ding-dongs of the old bell slowing down."

SILENCE IS GOLDEN

When Western Union asked Thomas Edison to "name his price" for the ticker he had invented, he asked for several days to consider it. His wife suggested $20,000, but he thought such an amount was exorbitant.

At the appointed time he went to the meeting still unsure as to his sales price. When the official asked, "How much?" he tried to say $20,000, but the words just wouldn't come out of his mouth. The official finally broke the silence and asked, "Well, how about $100,000?"

> I regret often that I have spoken; never that I have been silent. CYRUS

Often silence allows others to say something better than we could have said ourselves! By keeping quiet, others will have a greater interest in our thoughts; then when we have an interested audience, our words will have greater impact.

The Bible tells us that even a fool may be thought of as wise when his mouth is kept shut (Proverbs 17:28). In that sense, silence can keep us from embarrassing ourselves. People may think we are smarter than we really are.

When you feel moved to express an opinion, weigh the impact of your words and keep this thought in mind, "The less said, the best said." We can't get in trouble for what we don't say. Like Edison, we might even benefit from our silence.

When words are many, transgression is not lacking, but the prudent are restrained in speech.

PROVERBS 10:19 NRSV

☑ JUST DO IT

#1   It's been said that God gave us two ears and one mouth because He wants us to listen twice as much as we speak. Improve your listening skills with these six tips:

1. Maintain eye contact with the speaker.
2. Eliminate distractions.
3. Pay attention to nonverbal messages (e.g., facial expressions, tone of voice, posture, energy level).
4. Smile and nod your head to show interest in what the speaker is saying.
5. Think about what the speaker is saying, not just about what you are going to say next.
6. Put yourself in the speaker's shoes and try to understand how he/she feels.

Love never FAILS
[never fades out or becomes OBSOLETE or comes to an end].

I Corinthians 13:8 AMP

> There is no greater love than the love that holds on where there seems nothing left to hold on to.
>
> G.W.C. THOMAS

WHEN THE GOING GETS TOUGH

A family sailing trip almost turned into a tragedy when gale-force winds and towering waves threatened to swamp the family's vessel. Their frantic call to the Coast Guard brought two ships to their rescue. Unfortunately, the first ship had only a rope ladder, a means of evacuation too dangerous in such rough seas. Then the 900-foot tanker, James N. Sullivan, arrived. It shielded the sailboat until, after several hours of maneuvering, a set of stairs could be lowered from the side of the tanker to the sailboat.

Using a safety line, Bob and Sherry made the transfer in good order, as did their two young children. Then it was Grandmother Laurie's turn. Grandfather Dave passed her tether to Bob, but her harness got caught when she stepped across to the ladder. As the boats pulled apart, Laurie fell into the sea. With a surge of the waves, the boats came crashing back together. Dave was afraid to look—he knew that his beloved wife of thirty-three years could not swim, and even worse, he feared she might have been crushed as the boats collided. Nevertheless, he clung to the tether, refusing to let go. Grandmother later explained, "That's the only reason I'm here."

No matter how troubled the seas of life may become, hold on to the tether with your love. A life will be saved because you trusted God for the impossible!

Who's Who:

George Mueller

In November of 1844, George Mueller, the great Christian social reformer, began to pray for the salvation of five individuals. Later in life, he wrote in his diary:

I prayed [for them] every day without a single intermission, whether sick or in health, on the land, on the sea, and whatever the pressure of my engagements might be. Eighteen months elapsed before the first of the five was converted. I thanked God and prayed on for the others. Five years elapsed, and then the second was converted. I thanked God for the second, and prayed on for the other three. Day by day, I continued to pray for them, and six years passed before the third was converted. I thanked God for the three, and went on praying for the other two.

Fifty-two years after he started praying, the final two men were saved—after Mueller had died. What a beautiful example Mueller is to us today to never give up on those we love!

read more about it...worry

- *Finding Peace: God's Promise of a Life Free from Regret, Anxiety, and Fear*
  by Charles Stanley

- *Anxiety Attacked*
  by John MacArthur, Jr.

- *In Pursuit of Peace: 21 Ways to Conquer Anxiety, Fear, and Discontentment*
  by Joyce Meyer

- *From Worry to Worship: A 30-day Devotional Guide*
  by Julie Morris

- *Fearless: Building a Faith That Overcomes Your Fear*
  by Cheri Fuller

- *Straight Talk on Worry: Overcoming Emotional Battles with the Power of God's Word!*
  by Joyce Meyer

WHY WORRY?

A MILITARY CHAPLAIN once drew up a "Worry Table" based upon the problems men and women had brought to him through his years of service. He found their worries fit into these categories:

- Worries about things that never happened—40 percent
- Worries about past, unchangeable decisions—30 percent
- Worries about illness that never happened—12 percent
- Worries about adult children and friends (who were able to take care of themselves)—10 percent
- Worries about real problems—8 percent

According to his chart, 92 percent of all worries are about things we can't control, concerns which are better left to God. The truth is, most of our anxieties are rooted in a failure to trust God.

We simply don't believe He is big enough or cares enough to handle our problems, give us the desires of our hearts, and keeps us—and our loved ones—from harm.

Knowing God's character, we can easily see how we worry for nothing most of the time!

> **I've suffered** a great many catastrophes in my life. Most of them never happened.
>
> MARK TWAIN

God hath not given us the spirit of fear; but of power, and of love, and of a sound mind.

2 TIMOTHY 1:7 KJV

SISTERS OF THE HEART

> FRIENDSHIP IMPROVES **HAPPINESS, AND** ABATES MISERY, **BY DOUBLING** OUR JOY, AND **DIVIDING OUR** GRIEF.

THEY CALL themselves the "Ladies of the Lake," but they never set out to be a club. Rather, the group began when one of the women returned home exhausted from a business trip and came to the conclusion that she had too much of one thing in her life: MEN! With a husband and two boys at home, a work environment that was mostly male, and an elderly father and uncle to care for, she resolved to set some time aside for herself and a few female friends.

Over the years, Paula hadn't cultivated very many friendships with other women, but she was determined to see that change. Eventually she discovered three like-minded women: one owned a machine shop, one worked for a contractor, and one ran a truck stop. The women pulled out their calendars over dinner one evening and agreed on this schedule—"A trip to the lake at least once a quarter!"

At the lake, the women would listen to Mozart, fix gourmet dinners, and sit on the deck overlooking the water. They would talk for hours—about everything—without an agenda.

Over the years, they became very close and often refer to each other as "sister." Says Paula, "Nobody understands like another woman."

A **friend** loves at all times, and
a **brother** is born for **adversity.**

PROVERBS 17:17 NIV

TOP **10** TIPS

for Being
a Great Friend

1. TREAT YOUR FRIENDS THE WAY YOU WANT TO BE TREATED.

2. ALWAYS KEEP CONFIDENCES THAT ARE TOLD TO YOU.

3. BE A GOOD LISTENER; REFRAIN FROM OFFERING ADVICE UNLESS ASKED.

4. **FOLLOW THROUGH ON PLANS.**

5. BE VULNERABLE WITH YOUR FRIEND.

6. SUPPORT YOUR FRIEND THROUGH HARD TIMES AND BE WILLING TO ACCEPT HER SUPPORT WHEN YOU NEED IT.

7. MAKE TIME FOR YOUR FRIEND.

8. REJOICE IN YOUR FRIEND'S ACCOMPLISHMENTS.

9. DON'T GOSSIP WITH YOUR FRIEND.

10. **SHARE YOUR FAITH WITH YOUR FRIEND.**

LOVE SEES WHAT'S REAL

One Christmas morning, little Amy was delighted to find a beautiful golden-haired doll among the presents she unwrapped. "She's so pretty!" Amy squealed in excitement as she hugged her new doll. Then rushing to hug her grandmother, the giver of the doll, she cried, "Thank you, thank you, thank you!"

Amy played with her new doll most of the day, but toward evening she put it down and sought out one of her old dolls. Amy cradled the tattered and dilapidated old doll in her arms. Its hair had nearly worn away, its nose was broken, one eye was askew, and an arm was missing.

"Well, well," Grandma noted, "it seems as though you like that old dolly better."

"I like the beautiful doll you gave me, Grandma," little Amy explained, "but I love this old doll more, because if I didn't love her, no one else would."

We all know the saying, "Beauty is in the eye of the beholder." A similar saying might be, "Love is the choice of the beholder." When we see faults in others, we can choose to look beyond them. We can choose to love them regardless of their negative attributes, faults, or quirks.

LOVE SEES THROUGH A TELESCOPE NOT A MICROSCOPE.

LOVE ENDURES LONG AND IS PATIENT AND KIND. . . .
IT TAKES NO ACCOUNT OF THE EVIL DONE TO IT
[IT PAYS NO ATTENTION TO A SUFFERED WRONG].

1 CORINTHIANS 13:4,5 AMP

WISE WORDS

"Real isn't how you are made," said the Skin Horse. "It's a thing that happens to you. When a child loves you for a long, long time, not just to play with, but REALLY loves you, then you become Real."

"Does it hurt?" asked the Rabbit.

"Sometimes," said the Skin Horse, for he was always truthful. "When you are Real you don't mind being hurt."

"Does it happen all at once, like being wound up," he asked, "or bit by bit?"

"It doesn't happen all at once," said the Skin Horse. "You become. It takes a long time. That's why it doesn't often happen to people who break easily, or have sharp edges, or who have to be carefully kept. Generally, by the time you are Real, most of your hair has been loved off, and your eyes drop out, and you get loose in the joints and very shabby. But these things don't matter at all, because once you are Real you can't be ugly, except to people who don't understand."

FROM *THE VELVETEEN RABBIT* BY MARGERY WILLIAMS

CONSIDER
THIS!

It seems to be a universal truth that every child must plant a bean in a paper cup filled with soil and watch it sprout before he or she can leave elementary school. Do you remember doing that when you were a child as a simple elementary school science experiment? Perhaps you also remember that the sprout always grew toward the sun. You could turn the cup in any direction, and the sprout would soon reorient itself to face the sun. The life of the sprout thrived in the sunlight.

Likewise, people grow and thrive in the "sunlight" of consistent, sincere praise and encouragement. So don't keep positive comments to yourself in the dark. Throw open the windows of your heart and let praise spill forth like sunshine. You never know what tender young sprout you'll be nurturing and encouraging to become a mighty oak!

BUILD EACH OTHER UP

Everyone has an invisible sign hanging from his neck saying, "Make me feel important!"

It Isn't Enough

It isn't enough to say in our hearts
That we like a man for his ways,
It isn't enough that we fill our minds
With paeans of silent praise;
Nor is it enough that we honor a man
As our confidence upward mounts,
It's going right up to the man himself,
And telling him so that counts!
If a man does a work you really admire,
Don't leave a kind word unsaid,
In fear that to do so might make him vain
And cause him to "lose his head."
But reach out your hand and tell him,
"Well done," and see how his gratitude swells;
It isn't the flowers we strew on the grave,
It's the word to the living that tells.

—ANONYMOUS

For lack of praise, many think others draw negative conclusions about them. We can actually wound people by withholding our praise. Let someone know you think well of him or her today. What a difference your words will make!

Therefore **encourage** one another and **build** each other up, just as in fact you are doing.

I Thessalonians 5:11 NIV

SMALL DEEDS BRING GREAT RESULTS

A missionary was sailing home on furlough when she heard a cry one night—a cry that is perhaps the most difficult to hear when at sea: "Man overboard!" She arose quickly from her berth, lit the lamp on the bracket in her cabin, and then held the lamp at the window of her cabin in hopes of seeing some sign of life in the murky dark waters outside.

> **The smallest** deed is better than the greatest intention!

Seeing nothing she hung the lamp back on its bracket, snuffed it out, and returned to her berth with prayers for the man lost at sea. In the morning, to her surprise she discovered the man had been rescued. Not only that, but she learned it was the flash of her lamp through the porthole that showed those on deck the location of the missing man, who was clinging desperately to a rope still attached to the deck. He was pulled from the cold waters in the nick of time. Such a small deed as shining a lamp at the right time had saved a man's life.

It isn't the size of the deed you do that counts. It's the fact that you do it for good and not for evil, and with a trust that God can take every deed we perform and use it for His purposes, in our lives and in the lives of others.

Let us not **love** [merely] in **theory** or in speech but in **deed** and in truth [in practice and in **sincerity**].

1 JOHN 3:18 AMP

☑ JUST DO IT

#1   Keep a file folder and call it your "sunshine file." Whenever you get a note from someone thanking you for a kindness rendered, put it into the file. Whenever you hear from someone that something you did made a difference in his or her life, or the life of someone else, make a note about that and put it into the file.

    Then, on days when you may be feeling that you've contributed very little to the world, read through your "sunshine file." This effort is intended to do more than just provide you with a pat on the back. It will also remind you that little things mean a lot—little words of encouragement, little acts of kindness. It should put you in the habit of doing good to others and noticing, with thanksgiving, when others do good things for you. What a wonderful way to live in the Kingdom of God.

THE FIVE "DIGITS" OF PRAYER

MANY CHILDREN LEARN to count on their fingers, but a nurse once taught a child to pray on his fingers. This was her method:

Your thumb is the digit nearest to your heart, so pray first for those who are closest to you. Your own needs, of course, should be included, as well as those of your beloved family and friends.

The second finger is the one used for pointing. Pray for those who point you toward the truth, whether at church or school. Pray for your teachers, mentors, pastors, and those who inspire your faith.

The third finger is the tallest. Let it stand for the leaders in every sphere of life. Pray for those in authority—both within the body of Christ and those who hold office in various areas of government.

The fourth finger is the weakest, as every pianist knows. Let it stand for those who are in trouble and pain—the sick, injured, abused, wounded, or hurt.

The little finger is the smallest. Let it stand for those who often go unnoticed, including those who suffer abuse and deprivation.

What a simple and wonderful reminder as we pray! What a great tool to use in teaching children how to pray for themselves and others.

lighten up

A mom tells a story about saying bedtime prayers with her little girl. First the little girl listed all the things she was thankful for—including ketchup. Then she listed all the things she wanted God to do—including making her brother be nice to her. Finally, as an afterthought, she added, "Oh yeah, God, if there's anything I can do for You, just let me know."

> "Daily **prayers** will diminish your **cares.**"
>
> BETTY MILLS

cry aloud, and He shall hear my voice. PSALM 55:17 NKJV

"Be like a postage stamp— STICK to one thing till you get there."

JOSH BILLINGS

> Be steadfast, immovable, always abounding in the work of the Lord, knowing that your toil is not in vain in the Lord.
>
> 1 CORINTHIANS 15:58 NASB

PERSEVERANCE PAYS OFF

All her life, Veronica worked in jobs that served other people but gave her little personal satisfaction. As a young girl, she missed a lot of school to take care of her younger siblings and help with the family business. Consequently, she never learned to read.

After getting married, she worked as a cook in a restaurant, memorizing ingredient labels and recipes to conceal her illiteracy. Every day she lived in fear of making a mistake, while dreaming of one day being able to read.

A serious illness put Veronica in the hospital and then at home for a long recovery. Her health improved some, but not enough for her to go back to work. She saw this time as her opportunity to learn to read and enrolled in the adult reading program.

Veronica's new reading skills boosted her confidence, and she got involved in her church and in organizing community activities. She wrote a prize-winning cookbook and became a local celebrity.

Veronica never let go of her dream while working hard wherever she found herself. In the end, her dreams were realized far beyond her imagination!

Who's Who:

Haggai

The year was 538 B.C. A small remnant of the Jewish people had returned to their devastated homeland after being exiled for more than 50 years in Babylon. Their first task was to rebuild the temple. Enthusiastic at first, they worked to lay the temple's foundation. But their enthusiasm soon dwindled. The people became discouraged as they realized that the new temple would be far inferior to the one before, the splendid temple that Solomon built. Why even try, when their work would be a poor substitute for the original?

Then the prophet Haggai delivered these words of encouragement to them from God: "Be strong, all you people of the land," declares the Lord, "and work. For I am with you" (Haggai 2:4). How these words must have rung out in the hearts and minds of the discouraged Jewish people.

When you get discouraged in whatever you have been called to do—big or small—take heart! God is with you. Just be strong, work, and leave the result to Him.

Trivia

How to Say "I Love You"

Cantonese (Chinese-)--Moi oiy neya
Czech---Miluji te
Danish---Jeg elsker dig
French---Je t'aime
Italian---Ti amo
Sioux---Techihhila

A KISS A DAY

The **best** way to **hold** a
man is in your **arms.**

This old childhood rhyme is one that many people remember:

Kiss and hug,
Kiss and hug,
Kiss your sweety
On the mug.

While the rhyme was one children would use in ridiculing the puppy-love behavior of their older brothers and sisters, the practice of kissing and hugging actually has many healthful benefits beyond those of building a loving relationship.

A West German magazine reported the results of a study conducted by a life insurance company. The researchers discovered that husbands who kiss their wives every morning:

- live an average of five years longer,
- are involved in fewer automobile accidents,
- are ill 50 percent less, as noted by sick days, and
- earn 20 to 30 percent more money.

Other researchers have found that kissing and hugging releases endorphins, giving mind and body a sense of genuine well-being that is translated into better health.

A kiss a day just may keep the doctor away!

The man should give his wife
all that is her right as a married
woman, and the wife should do
the same for her husband.

1 CORINTHIANS 7:3 TLB

TRY A LITTLE TENDERNESS

Mentor Graham was so absorbed in evaluating assignments, he failed to notice the youthful giant who slouched into his Illinois schoolroom one day after school. After his eyes had adjusted to the brightness of the late-afternoon sunshine, causing the husky young man to be in silhouette before him, he recognized the youth as a newcomer to the community. The lad already had a reputation for "whipping the daylights" out of all the local toughs.

Graham would have been justified in thinking, *What does he want here? Am I in danger?* Rather, he looked up and down the six-foot-four-inches of muscle and ignorance before him and of-

NOTHING IS SO STRONG AS GENTLENESS. NOTHING IS SO GENTLE AS REAL STRENGTH.

fered to help the lad with his reading. When the young man left the schoolroom an hour later, he had several books under his arm—a loan from Mentor Graham with a promise of more in the future.

Few people re-member Graham. He was a quiet man, simply willing to do his best for any student who came his way. His pupil, however, became far more famous. His name was Abraham Lincoln.

A kind, helpful response to others is often perceived by them as strength. It is this gentle strength to which we are drawn. When you think you find yourself in a touchy situation, try a gentle touch!

THOU HAST ALSO GIVEN ME THE SHIELD
OF THY SALVATION; AND THY RIGHT HAND HATH HOLDEN ME UP,
AND THY GENTLENESS HATH MADE ME GREAT.

PSALM 18:35 KJV

WISE WORDS

Do all the good you can,
by all the means you can,
in all the ways you can,
in all the places you can,
at all the times you can,
to all the people you can
and as long as you can.

JOHN WESLEY

HOW Do YOU MEASURE Up?

Test your "kindness quotient" with the following self-test:

1. When a friend needs someone to talk to NOW, you:
   A. Tell her you'll schedule her sometime next week.
   B. Give her the name of a good therapist.
   C. Drop everything to spend some time together.

2. When someone at church needs help moving, you:
   A. Pretend that you're invisible.
   B. Have a sudden attack of back strain.
   C. Volunteer not only to help but also to use your pickup truck.

3. When the sign-up sheet to prepare meals for shut-ins comes around, you:
   A. Make it into a paper airplane.
   B. Pass it on, saying that you already contributed—two years ago.
   C. Sign your name and add to your shopping list the things you need to make your famous chicken casserole.

4. When God evaluates the kindness you show to others, He says:
   A. "Come on—you can do better than that!"
   B. "Have you read the parable about going the second mile?"
   C. "Well done! When it comes to kindness, you are a good and faithful servant!"

KINDNESS IS
AS KINDNESS DOES

**EACH LOVING
ACT SAYS LOUD
AND CLEAR, "I
LOVE YOU. GOD
LOVES YOU. I CARE.
GOD CARES."**

JOYCE HEINRICH AND ANNETTEE LA PLACA

A warm-from-the-oven casserole taken to the home of a sick friend…

A bouquet of flowers from your garden given to a neighbor…

A thank-you note sent to the performers who did such an excellent job during a concert or play you attended…

A loaf of freshly baked cinnamon bread brought to the office for coffee break…

A box of cookies taken to the police station on Christmas Day to encourage those who are on duty during the holiday…

A call to ask with genuine care and concern, "How are you doing?"…

We may not think of these as acts of Christian witnessing, yet they are. Every act of lovingkindness reflects God's lovingkindness for His people. We give because Jesus Christ has so freely given His love to us. He is the example we follow.

Never dismiss an act of lovingkindness as being too small or inconsequential. God will magnify even our smallest deeds to reveal His love to others.

Beloved, let us **love** one **another,**
for love is of **God;** and everyone who
loves is **born** of God and **knows** God.

1 JOHN 4:7-8 NKJV

THE FREEDOM OF FORGIVENESS

LISA WAS SHOCKED WHEN she discovered that David had run up thousands of dollars on every one of their credit cards. Not only was she furious about the mountain of debt, she was frustrated with herself for not recognizing David's habit of compulsive spending.

In the days that followed she wondered if she could ever trust her husband again, and whether they would ever be able to get out of debt.

Rather than wait for something to happen, she took two bold steps. The first was to convince David he needed help, and the second was to seek out a financial planner. She learned if she carefully monitored family funds, they could be out of debt in a few years. This brought hope for the financial future of their marriage.

> **Forgiveness** is giving love when there is no reason to.

Another turnaround in their marriage came when David asked Lisa to forgive him. She found that forgiving David freed her to turn away from the matter of money and to focus on their relationship. She decided it was possible to love someone even though they had "messed up." Forgiving made trust possible again, and once trust was reestablished their marriage began to be healed.

Forgiveness turns the heart away from what was and is, to what can be. Is it time for you to take some bold steps? If love is your motive, be encouraged. Situations can change.

Jesus said, "Blessed are the merciful, for they shall obtain mercy."

MATTHEW 5:7 NKJV

new insights into ageless questions

Q **From time to time it's good for all of us to evaluate how we're doing in the area of separating our needs from our wants. How would you honestly respond to the following questions?**

When I go shopping, I often:
A) Buy only those things I really need.
B) Buy things just because they're trendy.
C) Buy things I really can't afford.

When I see what my friends have, I often:
A) Feel that I have to have the same thing.
B) Thank God for blessing them with something so nice.
C) Sulk and feel insecure.

If I realize that my clothes closet is too crammed, do I:
A) Look around the house for more closet space I can use?
B) Combine clothes onto the same hanger to make room?
C) Sort out some clothes to give to charity?

AN ENCOURAGING WORD

Many years ago a famous singer was contracted to perform at a Paris opera house. The event was sold out in a matter of days. The entire city was abuzz with anticipation. That night the hall was packed with stately dressed men and women eager to hear the much-admired musician. The house manager took the stage and announced, "Ladies and gentlemen, thank you for your enthusiastic support. I am afraid that, due to illness, the woman whom you've all come to hear will not be performing tonight. However, we have found a suitable substitute we hope will provide you with comparable entertainment."

> **Kind words** can be short and easy to speak, but their echoes are truly endless.
>
> MOTHER TERESA

The crowd groaned so loudly in its disappointment that few heard the singer's name. Frustration replaced excitement in the hall. The stand-in singer gave everything she had, but when her performance was over she was met with an uncomfortable silence rather than applause. Then, from the balcony, a child stood up and shouted, "Mommy, I think you are wonderful!"

The crowd immediately responded with a thunderous ovation.

Once in a while we each need to hear somebody say, "I think you are wonderful." Why not be the person who gives that kind word of encouragement today!

She opens her mouth in skillful and godly Wisdom, and on her tongue is the law of kindness [giving counsel and instruction].

PROVERBS 31:26 AMP

JUST DO IT

to do | urgent

Encouraging Little Ones

Sometimes we forget that children need to be encouraged too —especially when they experience failure. The next time a child you're close to "stumbles" and needs encouragement to pick himself up, dust himself off, and start again, try these encouraging words:

- Making mistakes and learning from them is a part of growing up.
- Everybody makes mistakes—even Einstein made them!
- You're a great kid—you don't have to be perfect.
- Think about, and feel good about, what you did right.
- You may be embarrassed today, but tomorrow, I promise it won't feel so bad.
- Don't put yourself down—you can always try again.
- You're just like everyone else—good at some things and not so good at other things.
- No matter what, I love you and God loves you!

"**A** pint of **EXAMPLE** is worth a barrelful of **advice.**"

ANONYMOUS

Brethren, join in following my example, and observe those who walk according to the pattern you have in us.

PHILIPPIANS 3:17 NASB

BE THE EXAMPLE

On the fourth Sunday of July, the descendants of Roberto and Raquel Beaumont celebrate "Offspring Day." They have been doing this since 1956, when Raquel gathered her five preteen children around the dinner table at their home in Lima, Peru. She placed a rose by the napkin of each daughter and a carnation by the napkin of each son.

Knowing in a few years her children would be going their separate ways, she told her children that the gifts she gave them on Offspring Day were not mere flowers, but a token of her true gift to them—time and love. Furthermore, she expected them to pass on those same gifts to their children. Through the years, Raquel was the best example of her message: she always had time and love for each of her children, who regularly sought her advice and encouragement.

On Offspring Day each year, the elders who gather offer words of wisdom to their children. The young are encouraged to pick one thing about themselves they hope to improve in the coming year. It is a time for the generations to hear from one another and to set new goals for relationships. They do it all in the spirit of "Raquel's example."

Who's Who:

The Bible

God in His wisdom put the stories of many real people in the Bible to serve as examples for us. And so we have Moses to give us the example of stepping outside of our comfort zone. We have Abraham to give us the example of following wherever God leads. We have Naomi's example of faithfulness and Esther's example of courage, not to mention Job's example of perseverance.

Like these people God chose, we can be examples to our children and all those with whom we come into contact. Like them, we just have to be willing to let God use us in His way for our day.

TAKE YOURSELF LIGHTLY

A GOOD LAUGH IS SUNSHINE IN A HOUSE.

PEGGY WAS nervous about the upcoming dinner party she and her husband were about to host. It was their first time to have guests for dinner since the birth of their son, Pete. To top off Peggy's tension, the guests included her husband Bill's new supervisor.

Sensing the tension in his parents, the baby became irritable and fussy, which only added to Peggy's frustration. In an attempt to comfort little Pete, Peggy picked him up, raised him high over her head, and kissed his bare tummy. To her surprise, he smiled and giggled—the first genuine laugh she had heard from her young son.

In an instant, the evening took on an entirely new tenor. Peggy became more relaxed, and Baby Pete relaxed as well. The dinner party was a great success.

Can the laughter of a little child change a day? Yes! So can the laughter shared between two adults, or the chuckle prompted by the memory of a funny event.

When you're feeling stressed out, don't allow yourself to explode in anger. Get alone if you have to; but find a reason to laugh, and watch the stress melt away!

The light in the eyes
[of him whose heart is joyful]
rejoices the heart of others.

PROVERBS 15:30 AMP

TOP 10 TIPS

for Relieving Stress

1. LISTEN TO A RELAXING CD OF INSTRUMENTAL PRAISE MUSIC.

2. LIGHT SCENTED CANDLES AND TAKE A LONG, HOT BUBBLE BATH.

3. TAKE A WALK AND NOTE GOD'S WONDERFUL CREATIONS OF NATURE THAT YOU ENCOUNTER.

4. CALL YOUR BEST FRIEND AND HAVE A LONG CHAT.

5. GIVE YOURSELF A PEDICURE.

6. TAKE A GOOD BOOK TO A COFFEE SHOP. ENJOY IT WITH A LATTE.

7. WATCH A "CHICK FLICK," CURLED UP WITH A WARM AFGHAN AND BIG BOWL OF POPCORN.

8. WORK ON YOUR FAVORITE CRAFT.

9. SPLURGE—GET A DOUBLE DIP OF YOUR FAVORITE ICE CREAM FLAVOR.

10. READ A FEW PSALMS AND SPEND TIME TALKING WITH GOD.

booklist

OPEN HEART, OPEN HOME

IN *LITTLE HOUSE IN the Ozarks*, Laura Ingalls Wilder writes, "I spent an afternoon a short time ago with a friend in her new home. The house was beautiful and well-furnished with new furniture, but it seemed bare and empty to me. I wondered why this was until I remembered my experience with my new house. I could not make the living room seem homelike. I would move the chairs here and there and change the pictures on the wall, but something was lacking. Nothing seemed to change the feeling of coldness and vacancy that displeased me whenever I entered the room.

> **A house** is made of walls and beams; a home is made of love and dreams.

"Then, as I stood in the middle of the room one day wondering what I could possibly do to improve it, it came to me that all that was needed was for someone to live in it and furnish it with the everyday, pleasant thoughts of friendship and cheerfulness and hospitality."

A homey atmosphere is not a matter of the right decorations; it emanates from the thoughts and feelings of the people who live there. Feelings of warmth and welcome can be created only by people who are kind, generous, and even-tempered. Why not determine to "warm up" the atmosphere where you live today?

Better a **meal** of vegetables
where there is **love**
than a fattened calf with hatred.

PROVERBS 15:17 NIV

TAKING TIME FOR GOD

In *A Closer Walk*,[9] Catherine Marshall writes about a neighbor, "Cynthia felt she was losing her identity in an endless procession of social events and chauffeuring of children. During one cocktail party, Cynthia decided to limit herself to ginger ale and made some discoveries—not especially pleasant: 'I saw our crowd through new eyes,' she told me. 'No one was really saying anything. . . . All at once I began to ask questions about what we call 'the good life.'"

"In a search for answers, Cynthia set aside an hour each day for meditation. As she did this over a period of weeks there came to her the realization that she was being met in this quiet hour by something more than her own thoughts and psyche. . . . By Someone who loved her and insisted this love be passed on to her family and friends."

Cynthia made changes in her life as the result of her "hour with God." She turned meal times into a time for family sharing. Family Game Night became a substitute for television once a week. She and her husband joined a Bible study that met twice a month. In all, Cynthia concluded, "God . . . the Author of creativity, is ready to make a dull life adventuresome the moment we allow His Holy Spirit to go to work."

> YOU CAN ACCOMPLISH MORE IN ONE HOUR WITH GOD THAN ONE LIFETIME WITHOUT HIM.

WALK IN WISDOM . . . REDEEMING THE TIME.

COLOSSIANS 4:5 KJV

WISE WORDS

In the silence of the heart
God speaks. If you face God
in prayer and silence, God will
speak to you. Then you will
know that you are nothing.
It is only when you realize your
nothingness, your emptiness,
that God can fill you with
himself. Souls of prayer are
souls of great silence.

MOTHER TERESA

CONSIDER THIS!

When Dr. Wilfred Funk, well-known dictionary publisher, was asked to list the ten most expressive words in the English language, he provided the following list:

- The most bitter word—alone.
- The most tragic word—death.
- The most revered word—mother.
- The most beautiful word—love.
- The most cruel word—revenge.
- The most peaceful word—tranquil.
- The saddest word—forgotten.
- The warmest word—friendship.
- The coldest word—no.
- The most comforting word—faith.

Remember, words are full of meaning, so choose yours with care!

WORDS THAT WOUND

STACK EVERY BIT OF CRITICISM BE-TWEEN TWO LAYERS OF PRAISE.

Shortly after graduation, Joe and Lana married. One of their first marital discoveries was their very different understanding of "being on time." Not wanting to end the honeymoon stage too early, Lana found herself mildly complaining about Joe's being late. But Joe never took the hint, and soon her complaining turned to outright criticism.

On the surface, there may not seem to be much difference between exposing a problem and criticizing, but in a relationship, the choice of words can bring very different responses. Criticism attacks someone's personality and character. When Lana criticized Joe, she would say, "You're only thinking about yourself!"

Putting an issue on the table for discussion in a positive manner is the first step toward finding a resolution. A person who asks gently, "Does it embarrass you when we are late?" is opening a dialog for finding the solution to the problem. Criticism only wounds the spirit, puts the other person on the defensive, and usually ends up in a no-resolution argument.

Watch what you say! Criticism can cause a wound that takes years to heal, but a kind and gracious attitude in problem-solving can save you years of tears.

Correct, rebuke and encourage—with great patience and careful instruction.

2 TIMOTHY 4:2 NIV

WHAT'S IN A NAME?

In 1955 the city buses in Montgomery, Alabama, were segregated by law. White people and black people were not allowed to sit together.

On December 1 of that year, Mrs. Rosa Parks was riding the bus home from her job at a tailor shop. As the section for whites filled up, the black people were ordered to move to the back to make room for the white passengers who were boarding. Three blacks in Mrs. Parks' row moved, but Mrs. Parks remained in her seat. Later she said, "Our mistreatment was just not right, and I was tired of it. I knew someone had to take the first step. So I made up my mind not to move."

The bus driver asked her if she was going to stand up. "No, I am not," she answered him. Mrs. Parks was arrested and taken to jail. Four days later black people and white sympathizers organized a boycott of the city bus line that lasted until a year later, when the Supreme Court declared the segregated-bus ordinance unconstitutional.

Mrs. Parks is known today as the "mother of the modern-day civil rights movement." Her name inspires others to be courageous and do what is right, despite the circumstances.

> **Being held** in high esteem is better than having silver or gold.
>
> PROVERBS 22:1 NLT

If you were given a **nickname** descriptive of your **character**, would you be **proud** of it?

#1

It's always interesting to hear how people are named in other cultures. Often the exercise of naming is far more creative than looking in a book of baby names. For instance, the Native Americans named those in their tribe according to conditions like the phases of the moon or the geographic location of the baby's birth. Thus they might choose names like "Rising Moon" or "Raging River."

Think of those in your family and circle of close friends and neighbors. If you were going to give each one a new name that reflects his or her deeds or characteristics, what would those names be? Would someone be "she who always smiles" or "he who tells jokes"? If the names you think of are flattering, share them as an encouragement to those you know!

#2

#3

#4

#5

#6

#7

#8

#9

#10

Trivia

As we admire the flowers and let them speak to us of the "bonus beauty" God has put in the world, it's sometimes fun to think about the characteristics or attributes with which different flowers are traditionally associated. Match the flowers in the list below with the attribute for which they stand.

1. Rose
2. White Lily
3. Pansy
4. Peony
5. Violet
6. Marigold

a. Thoughts
b. Bashfulness
c. Purity
d. Love
e. Grief
f. Faithfulness

(Answers: 1d, 2c, 3a, 4b, 5f, 6e.)

LIFE'S LITTLE EXTRAS

Life is not a **problem** to be solved,
but a gift to be **enjoyed**.

JOSEPH P. DOOLEY

The fictional character Sherlock Holmes is known for his keen power of observation in solving crimes. But Holmes also used his observation skills in renewing his faith. In *The Adventure of the Naval Treaty*, Dr. Watson says of Holmes: "He walked past the couch to an open window and held up the drooping stalk of a moss rose, looking down at the dainty blend of crimson and green. It was a new phase of his character to me, for I had never before seen him show an interest in natural objects.

"'There is nothing in which deduction is so necessary as in religion,' said he, leaning with his back against the shutters. . . . 'Our highest assurance of the goodness of Providence seems to me to rest in the flowers. All other things, our powers, our desires, our food, are really necessary for our existence in the first instance. But this rose is an extra. Its smell and its color are an embellishment of life, not a condition of it. It is only goodness which gives extras, and so I say again that we have much to hope from the flowers.'"[10]

Life is filled with extras—gifts from a loving God that embellish and enrich our lives. Take time to observe some of them today!

This is the day the Lord has
made; let us rejoice
and be glad in it.

PSALM 118:24 NIV

"You cannot do a kindness **TOO SOON,** because you never know how soon it will be **too late.**"

Anonymous

LITTLE KINDNESSES MAKE BIG IMPRESSIONS

William McKinley served in Congress before he was elected the twenty-fifth President of the United States. On his way to his congressional office one morning, he boarded a streetcar and took the only remaining seat. Minutes later, a woman who appeared to be ill boarded the car. Unable to find a seat, she clutched an overhead strap next to one of McKinley's colleagues. The other congressman hid behind his newspaper and did not offer the woman his seat. McKinley walked up the aisle, tapped the woman on the shoulder, offered her his seat, and took her place in the aisle.

Years later when McKinley was President, this same congressman was recommended to him for a post as ambassador to a foreign nation. McKinley refused to appoint him. He feared a man who didn't have the courtesy to offer his seat to a sick woman in a crowded streetcar would lack the courtesy and sensitivity necessary to be an ambassador in a troubled nation. The disappointed congressman bemoaned his fate to many in Washington, but never did learn why McKinley chose someone else for the position.

Acts of kindness can lead you to prominence. Then, from that position of prominence, you can be kind to even more people.

Who's Who:

Ruth Bell Graham

When Jim Bakker, well-known televangelist and president of the PTL organization, was convicted of fraud, he was sent to prison for his crime for almost five years. Not long after he was released, he was invited to dinner at the home of Billy and Ruth Bell Graham.

Jim recalls that sometime during that evening, Ruth asked him a question that required him to look up an address. He reached into his back pocket and pulled out an envelope. His wallet had been taken when he went to prison, and he had not owned one since.

As he fumbled through the envelope for the address, Ruth asked him, "Don't you have a wallet, Jim?" Jim replied that the envelope was his "wallet."

Ruth left the room and soon returned with one of her husband's wallets. She explained that it was a brand-new wallet and Billy had never used it. She handed the wallet to Jim, saying, "I want you to have it."

About the experience, Jim says, "I still carry that wallet to this day. Over the years I have met thousands of wonderful Christian men and women, but never anyone more humble, gracious, and in a word, 'real' than Ruth Graham and her family."

Often, it's our smallest expressions of kindness that make the biggest impressions on others.

HOW Do YOU MEASURE Up?

How Patient Are You?

1. When someone in front of me in the express line at the grocery store has more than the allotted items, I:
   A. Huff away to another line.
   B. Comment to the offender.
   C. Comment to the clerk.
   D. Patiently wait my turn.

2. When I'm stuck in traffic on the freeway, I:
   A. Switch lanes, constantly trying to get ahead.
   B. Drive down the shoulder to get to the next exit.
   C. Honk my horn at the people in front of me.
   D. Take a deep breath and use it as an opportunity to pray or listen to music.

3. When a child is acting up in church, I:
   A. Tap the mother on the shoulder and inform her of the nursery down the hall.
   B. Look for an usher and "give him the eye."
   C. Offer to take the child to the nursery myself.
   D. Ignore the disturbance and focus on worship.

PATIENCE PLEASE

> **IT'S EASY** TO IDENTIFY PEOPLE WHO CAN'T COUNT TO TEN. THEY'RE IN FRONT OF YOU IN THE SUPERMARKET EXPRESS LANE.
>
> JUNE HENDERSON

A woman once visited a friend in Cambridge, Massachusetts, home of several well-known institutions of higher learning. She accompanied the friend to a supermarket on Saturday afternoon, finding it crammed with shoppers and very long checkout lines.

While the two of them stood patiently in line, they noticed a college-age young man wheel a filled shopping cart into the cash register stall that was clearly marked, "Express Line—10 Items or Less."

The checkout girl of the express line looked at the loaded cart and then at the young man. He was trying to ignore her exasperated expression by fumbling for his checkbook in his knapsack.

Realizing she was stuck with a stubborn and inconsiderate customer, the girl said loudly to the high school student who was helping her bag groceries, "This guy either goes to Harvard and can't count, or he goes to M.I.T. and can't read!"

Although we don't always think of it in these terms, impatience reveals a selfish and often mean spirit, while patience is really an act of kindness.

Be **patient** with everyone.

1 THESSALONIANS 5:14 NIV

OVERLOOKING LITTLE IRRITATIONS

The story is told of a couple at their golden wedding anniversary celebration. Surrounded by her children, grandchildren, and great-grandchildren, the wife was asked the secret to a long and happy marriage. With a loving glance toward her husband, she answered: "On my wedding day, I decided to make a list of ten of my husband's faults which, for the sake of our marriage, I would overlook. I figured I could live with at least ten faults."

A guest asked her to identify some of the faults she had chosen to overlook. Her husband looked a bit troubled at the thought of having his foibles and flaws revealed to the assembled group. However, his wife sweetly replied, "To tell you the truth, dear, I never did get around to listing them. Instead, every time my husband did something that made me hopping mad, I would simply say to myself, *Lucky for him that's one of the ten!*"

Even the most devoted friends and spouses will experience storms in their relationships from time to time. Some problems are worth addressing in order to resolve them. Others are best left undiscussed. In time, issues of little importance tend to blow past without any need for "blowup."

> THE ART OF BEING WISE IS THE ART OF KNOWING WHAT TO OVERLOOK.
>
> WILLIAM JAMES

A MAN'S WISDOM GIVES HIM PATIENCE; IT IS TO HIS GLORY TO OVERLOOK AN OFFENSE.

PROVERBS 19:11 NIV

WISE WORDS

Oh, the comfort—the inexpressible comfort of feeling safe with a person, having neither to weigh thoughts, nor measure words, but pouring them all right out, just as they are, chaff and grain together, certain that a faithful hand will take and sift them, keep what is worth keeping—and with a breath of kindness, blow the rest away.

DINAH MARIE MULOCK CRAIK

WHAT'S YOUR LEGACY?

IN *GRAND ESSENTIALS*, BEN Patterson writes: "I have a theory about old age. . . . I believe that when life has whittled us down, when joints have failed and skin has wrinkled . . . what is left of us will be what we were all along, in our essence.

"Exhibit A is a distant uncle. . . . All his life he did nothing but find new ways to get rich. . . . He spent his senescence very comfortably, drooling and babbling constantly about the money he had made. . . . When life whittled him down to his essence, all there was left was raw greed.

"Exhibit B is my wife's grandmother. . . . The best example I can think of was when we asked her to pray before dinner. She would reach out and hold the hands of those sitting beside her, a broad, beatific smile would spread across her face, her dim eyes would fill with tears as she looked up to heaven, and her chin would quaver as she poured out her love to Jesus. That was Edna in a nutshell. She loved Jesus and she loved people. She couldn't remember our names, but she couldn't keep her hands from patting us lovingly whenever we got near her. When life whittled her down to her essence, all there was left was love: love for God and love for people."[11]

> **Beware lest** your footprints on the sand of time leave only the marks of a heel.

The **memory** of the righteous
will be a **blessing**, but the **name** of
the **wicked** will **rot**.

PROVERBS 10:7 NIV

Q I really don't have much money or anything of great value to leave my children and grandchildren. How can I leave them a legacy?

Maybe you don't think you're leaving a legacy of any value because you're looking at your worth through the world's eyes rather than God's eyes. Do you have a child who takes the same delight in Christmas as you and always wants to help decorate or bake? Chances are he or she will pass that tradition along to the next generation. Do you have a grandchild who gets your corny jokes before everyone else? It's possible that he or she inherited your unique sense of humor and will continue to bring joy throughout his or her life. What memories have you made with your family? What prayers have you prayed? What scripture verses have you shared? With whom have you laughed . . . and cried? All those things make up your true legacy—a legacy that comes from who you are, rather than what you have.

booklist

ALL ABOARD THE SUNSHINE TRAIN

A LITTLE GIRL WAS eating her breakfast one morning when a ray of sunlight suddenly appeared through the clouds and reflected off the spoon in her cereal bowl. She immediately put it into her mouth. With a big smile she exclaimed to her mother, "I just swallowed a spoonful of sunshine!"

A spoonful of sunshine just may be the best "soul food" that a person can have in a day. A prominent surgeon once wrote, "Encourage your child to be merry and to laugh aloud. A good, hearty laugh expands the chest and makes the blood bound merrily along. A good laugh will sound right through the house. It will not only do your child good, but will be a benefit to all who hear, and be an important means of driving the blues away from a dwelling. Merriment is very catching, and spreads in a remarkable manner, few being able to resist the contagion. A hearty laugh is delightful harmony; indeed it is the best of music."[12]

> The **most wasted** of all days is that on which one has not laughed.
>
> SEBASTIAN-ROCHE

An old poem advises: If you are on the gloomy line, the worry train, or the grouchy track, get a transfer! It's time to climb aboard the sunshine train and sit in one of its cheerful cars.

A **happy** heart makes the face cheerful, but heartache **crushes** the spirit.

PROVERBS 15:13 NIV

WINNING GOD'S WAY

Ruth Bell Graham tells a humorous story about her daughters, Anne and Bunny. When Ruth ran to the kitchen to investigate some loud cries, she found three-year-old Bunny holding her hand to her cheek, looking very disapprovingly at her sister. "Mommy," explained five-year-old Anne, "I'm teaching Bunny the Bible. I'm slapping her on one cheek and teaching her to turn the other one so I can slap it too."[13]

> **Silence is** one of the hardest arguments to refute.
>
> JOSH BILLINGS

When we are wronged, our first response is more likely to fight back than to turn the other cheek. But many have found that fighting back can be counterproductive.

Missionary E. Stanley Jones was being publicly slandered by someone he had once helped. Jones' first response was to write his accuser a letter he relates was "the kind of reply you are proud of the first five minutes, the second five minutes you're not so certain, and the third five minutes you know you're wrong."

Jones knew his comments would win the argument, but lose the person. "The Christian," he said, "is not in the business of winning arguments, but of winning people," and he tore up the letter. A few weeks later—without having said a word—Jones received a letter of apology from the one who had turned on him.

To watch over mouth and tongue is to keep out of trouble.

PROVERBS 21:23 NRSV

☑ JUST DO IT

#1   Try as we might to forgive a wrong, it's sometimes hard to really let it go when the pain is deep or the hurt is ongoing. Consider spilling out all your feelings into a letter to the one you believe has wronged you. Go ahead and list all the reasons you feel you are right and they are wrong. But whatever you do, don't send that letter.

    Sleep on it. Pray over it. Ask the Lord to illuminate any statement that needs to be reexamined, then burn the letter or tear it into little pieces. You'll find the exercise to be amazingly healing, helping you let go of the hurt once and for all but leaving room for God to bridge the gap between you and the person who hurt you.

THE SECRET OF TRUE HAPPINESS

> TO **LOVE** WHAT YOU DO AND FEEL THAT IT **MATTERS**— HOW COULD ANYTHING BE MORE **FUN?**
>
> CATHERINE GRAHAM

A NEWSPAPER IN England once asked this question of its readers, "Who are the happiest people on the earth?'

The four prize-winning answers were:

A little child building sand castles.

A craftsman or artist whistling over a job well done.

A mother bathing her baby after a busy day.

A doctor who has finished a difficult and dangerous operation that saved a human life.

The paper's editors were surprised to find virtually no one submitted kings, emperors, millionaires, or others of riches and rank as the happiest people on earth.

W. Beran Wolfe once said, "If you observe a really happy man you will find him building a boat, writing a symphony, educating his son, growing double dahlias in his garden, or looking for dinosaur eggs in the Gobi Desert. He will not be searching for happiness as if it were a collar button that has rolled under the radiator. He will not be striving for it as a goal in itself. He will have become aware that he is happy in the course of living life twenty-four crowded hours of the day."

When you eat the labor of your hands, You shall be happy, and it shall be well with you.

PSALM 128:2 NKJV

TOP **10** WAYS to Be Unhappy (Guaranteed)

1. LET LITTLE THINGS BOTHER YOU.

2. LOSE YOUR PERSPECTIVE OF WHAT'S REALLY IMPORTANT IN LIFE.

3. FIND SOMETHING TO WORRY ABOUT.

4. BE A PERFECTIONIST.

5. BE RIGHT, ALWAYS RIGHT, ALL THE TIME.

6. DON'T TRUST OR BELIEVE OTHER PEOPLE.

7. ALWAYS COMPARE YOURSELF UNFAVORABLY WITH OTHERS.

8. TAKE PERSONALLY EVERYTHING THAT HAPPENS TO YOU THAT YOU DON'T LIKE.

9. NEVER GIVE YOURSELF WHOLEHEARTEDLY TO ANYONE OR ANYTHING.

10. MAKE SELF-GRATIFICATION THE PRIMARY GOAL OF YOUR LIFE.

"Triumph is just 'UMPH' added to try."

ANONYMOUS

KEEP ON GOIN'

Monica Seles finally won a tennis tournament two years after she was stabbed in the shoulder by a crazed fan.

Withstanding one hundred-degree heat and tendonitis in her left knee, she roared through the Canadian Open to defeat three Top 20 players en route to a finals match that lasted only fifty-one minutes. Her nightmare recovery had truly come to an end.

To help in her recovery, Monica asked Olympic champion Jackie Joyner-Kersee and her coach/husband, Bob Kersee, to put her on a strict workout routine. While on this physical regimen she also worked to overcome the emotional problems that accompany such an attack.

Her father and coach, Karolj, who had been stricken by prostate and stomach cancer, was her continual source of inspiration. She said, "I was down and he came into my room and said he couldn't stand to see me that way. I decided then that I had to try and put it behind me and move on."

Have you ever felt "stabbed in the back" while doing good? Withdrawal is often our first temptation, but with a creative and loving God, who continually inspires us, we just can't quit! Our detractors will have to say about us what was said about Monica, "She's back!"

Who's Who:

Nichelle Nichols

Nichelle Nichols played the role of Uhura in the original Star Trek series. As one of the first African-American women regularly featured on a weekly television show, she faced many obstacles because of her race—the hostility of studio executives, script rewrites designed to diminish her role, even the withholding of her fan mail.

Nichelle was ready to give up, when she met Dr. Martin Luther King, who encouraged her not to leave the show as she was a positive role model for other African-American women. In an interview featured in USA Today, Nichelle said, "When you have a man like Dr. Martin Luther King say you can't leave a show, it's daunting. It humbled my heart, and I couldn't leave. God had charged me with something more important than my own career."

Nichelle did go on, despite the obstacles, and became an important influence for the cause of African-American women in our nation.

CONSIDER
THIS!

One morning, the owner of a drive-through coffee shop in Portland, Oregon, was surprised when one customer not only paid for his own coffee, but also paid for that of the person in the car behind him. The owner was pleased to be able to tell the next customer that her coffee had already been paid for. Then to her continued surprise, that second customer paid for the coffee of the next person in line.

The idea of one customer paying for the coffee of the next one in line caught on. The "string of kindness" went on for two hours, and twenty-seven customers participated!

CARING FOR OTHERS

On a bitter, cold Virginia evening, an old man waited on a path by a river, hoping for someone on a horse to carry him across. His beard was glazed with frost, and his body grew numb before he finally heard the thunder of horses' hooves. Anxiously he watched as several horsemen appeared. He let the first pass by without making an effort to get his attention, then another and another. Finally, only one rider remained. As he drew near, the old man caught his eye and asked, "Sir, would you mind giving me a ride to the other side?"

The rider helped the man onto his horse and, sensing he was half-frozen, decided to take him all the way home, which was several miles out of the way. As they rode, the horseman asked, "Why didn't you ask one of the other men to help you? I was the last one. What if I had refused?"

The old man said, "I've been around awhile, son, and I know people pretty well. When I looked into their eyes and saw they had no concern for my condition, I knew it was useless to ask. When I looked into your eyes, I saw kindness and compassion."

At the door of the old man's house the rider resolved, "May I never get too busy in my own affairs that I fail to respond to the needs of others." And with that, Thomas Jefferson turned and directed his horse back to the White House.

> **PEOPLE DON'T CARE HOW MUCH YOU KNOW, UNTIL THEY KNOW HOW MUCH YOU CARE. . . ABOUT THEM.**
>
> ZIG ZIGLAR

If I have prophetic powers, and understand all mysteries and all knowledge, and if I have all faith, so as to remove mountains, but do not have love, I am nothing.

1 CORINTHIANS 13:2 NRSV

AGAINST THE ODDS

Many years ago, a young woman who felt called to the ministry was accepted into a noted seminary. There were only two other women enrolled, and her very presence seemed to make her male classmates uncomfortable. She felt isolated, yet on display at the same time. To make matters worse, many of her professors were doing their best to destroy her faith rather than build it up. Even her private time of devotions seemed dry and lonely.

At Christmas break she sought her father's counsel. "How can I be strong in my resolve and straight in my theology with all that I face there?"

Her father took a pencil from his pocket and laid it on the palm of his hand. "Can that pencil stand upright by itself?" he asked her.

"No," she replied. Then her father grasped the pencil in his hand and held it in an upright position.

"Ah," she said, "but you are holding it now."

"Daughter," he replied, "your life is like this pencil. But Jesus Christ is the one who can hold you." The young woman took her pencil and returned to seminary.

> IT IS SUCH A COMFORT TO DROP THE TANGLES OF LIFE INTO GOD'S HANDS AND LEAVE THEM THERE.

CAST YOUR CARES ON THE LORD AND HE WILL SUSTAIN YOU.

PSALM 55:22 NIV

WISE WORDS

God entrusted women with some of
His most important tasks. He sent
women with the Resurrection news to
the rest of the disciples. Jesus accepted women into full discipleship. He
commended Mary of Bethany for her
efforts to sit at His feet and learn,
rather than do the accepted thing and
retire to the kitchen. To those who
say women cannot fill positions of
leadership, the Bible says women did.
As the great evangelist D. L. Moody
replied when someone asked him
what a woman can do to serve Christ,
"What could they not do?"

PATRICIA GUNDRY

Trivia

Africa is home to some of the world's most fascinating animals, including the impala, which can jump to a height of over 10 feet and, in the same jump, cover a distance of more than 30 feet. However, this amazing animal can be safely kept in a zoo, enclosed by a solid wall only three feet high. Why? Because an impala will not jump if it cannot see where its feet will land.

Life often requires us to take risks—to jump without knowing where our feet will land. Yet God often prompts our hearts to make such risky jumps, despite what others say. Fortunately, faith gives us the confidence we need to conquer our fear and jump. God doesn't want us to be limited by the small, three-feet-tall barriers in life. He desires for you to take hold of His hand and jump, trusting Him with all your heart and soul for the outcome.

TAKE A RISK IN FAITH

Life is a **coin**. You can **spend**
it **any way** you wish, but
you can **only** spend it **once**.

LILLIAN DICKSON

Anita Septimus has worked as a social worker for HIV-infected children since 1985. In the first few months she worked with her tiny clients, three of them died. Despair began to overwhelm her. She made a commitment to stick with the job for three more months, during which time she could not get a friend's words out of her thoughts: "You have not chosen a pretty profession."

She had to admit, her friend was right. It took resolve to accept that fact and simply do what she could to help families make the most of what remained of their children's lives. She is still there.

Over the last ten years, her clinic has grown considerably. Today, Anita and her staff care for more than three hundred families with AIDS children. They go into their homes, teach infection prevention, and help the parents plan for the future. The children are regularly taken on trips to the zoo, the circus, and summer camps.

One AIDS baby wasn't expected to see her first birthday, but she recently celebrated her tenth. Such "long-term" clients give back to Anita what she terms "an indestructible sense of hope"—a precious gift!

How do you **know** what will happen
tomorrow? For your **life**
is like the morning fog—it's here a
little while, then it's **gone.**

JAMES 4:14 NLT

BE NOT AFRAID

Napoleon called Marshall Ney the bravest man he had ever known. Yet Ney's knees trembled so badly one morning before a battle, he had difficulty mounting his horse. When he finally was in the saddle, he shouted contemptuously down at his limbs, "Shake away, knees. You would shake worse than that if you knew where I am going to take you."

Courage is not a matter of not being afraid. It is a matter of taking action even when you are afraid.

> **Courage** is resistance to fear, mastery of fear. Not the absence of fear. MARK TWAIN

Courage is also more than sheer bravado—shouting, "I can do this!" and launching out with a do-or-die attitude over some reckless dare.

True courage is manifest when a person chooses to take a difficult or even dangerous course of action because it is the right thing to do. Courage is looking beyond yourself to what is best for another.

The source of all courage is the Holy Spirit of God, our Comforter. It is His nature to remain by our side to help us. When we welcome Him into our lives and He compels us to do something, we can confidently trust He will be right there, helping us get it done.

Therefore, take up the full armor of God, that you will be able to resist in the evil day, and having done everything, to stand firm. Stand firm therefore.

Ephesians 6:13-14 NASB

☑ JUST DO IT

#1   There are many passages in the Bible that address the topic of fear. Write the following verses on small cards that you can carry in your purse or wallet. Then when you need a shot of courage, take them out, read them, and be reminded that God is with you always, even when you're feeling fearful.

- Joshua 1:9 NIV: *"Be strong and courageous. Do not be terrified; do not be discouraged, for the Lord your God will be with you wherever you go."*

- Psalm 27:1 NIV: *The Lord is my light and my salvation— whom shall I fear? The Lord is the stronghold of my life— of whom shall I be afraid?*

- Psalm 56:3 NIV: *When I am afraid, I will trust in you.*

- Mark 5:36 NIV: *Jesus said, "Don't be afraid; just believe."*

- Hebrews 13:4 NIV: *We say with confidence, "The Lord is my helper; I will not be afraid. What can man do to me?"*

booklist

- *Sacred Companions: The Gift of Spiritual Friendship & Direction*
  by David G. Brenner

- *The Friendships of Women*
  by Dee Brestin

- *The Red Hat Society™: Fun and Friendship after Fifty*
  by Sue Ellen Cooper

- *I Know Just What You Mean: The Power of Friendship in Women's Lives*
  by Ellen Goodman and Patricia O'Brien

- *In the Company of Women: Deepening Our Relationships with the Important Women in Our Lives*
  by Dr. Brenda Hunter

THE GIFT OF FRIENDSHIP

A WOMAN WAS IN A serious automobile accident in a city far from home. She felt so enclosed in a cocoon of pain, she didn't realize how lonely she was until a "forgotten" friend in the city came to visit her. She firmly but gently said to her, "You should not be alone."

In the weeks that followed, this friend's advice rang in the injured woman's ears and helped her to overcome her otherwise reserved nature. When another friend called from a city several hundred miles away to say she wanted to come stay with her, the injured woman didn't say, "Don't bother"—as would have been her normal response. Rather, she said, "Please come." The friend was a wonderful encourager and nurse to her, reading the Psalms aloud when she was still too weak to read herself. Then yet another friend offered to come and help in her recovery. Again she swallowed her pride and said, "Please do." This friend stayed for several months until the injured woman was able to care for herself.

Even Jesus did not carry His own cross all the way to Calvary. He allowed another to help shoulder His burden. It's all right to ask for help and to receive help. You don't have to "go it alone." Let a friend help you.

> **The best antique is an old friend.**

Your own friend and your father's friend, forsake them not. . . . Better is a neighbor who is near [in spirit] than a brother who is far off [in heart].

PROVERBS 27:10 AMP

DON'T GIVE UP!

Somebody said that it couldn't be done,
But he with a chuckle replied,
That "maybe it couldn't" but he would be one
Who wouldn't say so till he'd tried.
So he buckled right in with the trace of a grin
On his face. If he worried, he hid it.
He started to sing as he tackled the thing
That couldn't be done. And he did it.
Somebody scoffed: "Oh, you'll never do that,
    At least no one ever has done it."
    But he took off his coat and took off his hat
    And the first thing he knew he'd begun it.
    With the lift of his chin and a bit of a grin,
    If any doubt rose he forbid it;
    He started to sing as he tackled the thing
    That couldn't be done, and he did it.
    There are thousands to tell you
it cannot be done,
There are thousands to prophesy failure;
There are thousands to point out to you,
one by one,
The dangers that wait to assail you,
But just buckle right in with a bit of a grin,
Then take off your coat and go to it.
Just start in to sing as you tackle the thing
That cannot be done, and you'll do it.
—Edgar A. Guest

> **In trying**
> times,
> don't quit
> trying.

Don't get tired of doing what is good.
Don't get discouraged and give up, for we will reap
a harvest of blessing at the appropriate time.

GALATIANS 6:9 NLT

What can I do to become deeply rooted in my faith so that I can endure hard times?

Putting down deep roots will require that you go beyond the surface and deal with spiritual issues that are inside you, hidden from sight. That's a tough assignment. It may mean dealing with wrong motives or selfish ambitions. It could mean giving or receiving forgiveness in painful situations. Most of all, it means coming clean with yourself and God as you are led by the Holy Spirit. It isn't easy—but it's worth it. The deep roots you will develop will keep you strong and well-watered and thriving regardless of what unpleasant circumstance comes your way.

BETTER KIND THAN RIGHT

In looking over a café menu, a woman noticed that both a chicken salad sandwich and a chicken sandwich were listed. She decided to order the chicken salad sandwich, but absentmindedly wrote "chicken sandwich" on her order slip. When the waiter brought the chicken sandwich, she protested immediately, insisting the waiter had erred.

Most waiters would have picked up the order slip and shown the customer the mistake she had made. But instead he expressed regret at the error, picked up the sandwich, returned to the kitchen, and a moment later placed a chicken salad sandwich in front of the woman.

While eating her sandwich, the woman picked up her order slip and noticed the mistake she had made. When it was time to pay for the meal, she apologized to the waiter and offered to pay for both sandwiches. The waiter said, "No, Ma'am. That's perfectly all right. I'm just happy you've forgiven me for being right."

> TACT IS THE ART OF MAKING A POINT WITHOUT MAKING AN ENEMY.
>
> DR. JOHN OLSON

RECKLESS WORDS PIERCE LIKE A SWORD, BUT THE TONGUE OF THE WISE BRINGS HEALING.

PROVERBS 12:18 NIV

WISE WORDS

Kind words are the music of the world.
They have a power which seems to be
beyond natural causes, as if they were
some angel's song which had lost its way
and come on earth. It seems as if they
could almost do what in reality God alone
can do—soften the hard and angry hearts
of men. No one was ever corrected by
sarcasm—crushed, perhaps, if the sarcasm was clever enough, but drawn near-
er to God, never.

FREDERICK WILLIAM FABER

"My obligation is to do the RIGHT thing. The rest is in God's hands."

MARTIN LUTHER KING JR.

> If you know that he is righteous, you may be sure that everyone who does right is born of him.
>
> 1 JOHN 2:29 RSV

DO YOUR PART

In *Dakota,* Kathleen Norris writes: "A Benedictine sister from the Philippines once told me what her community did when some sisters took to the streets in the popular revolt against Marcos' regime. Some did not think it proper for nuns to demonstrate in public, let alone risk arrest. In a group meeting that began and ended with prayer, the sisters who wished to continue demonstrating explained that this was for them a religious obligation; those who disapproved also had their say. Everyone spoke; everyone heard and gave counsel.

"It was eventually decided that the nuns who were demonstrating should continue to do so; those who wished to express solidarity but were unable to march would prepare food and provide medical assistance to the demonstrators, and those who disapproved would pray for everyone. The sisters laughed and said, 'If one of the conservative sisters was praying that we young, crazy ones would come to our senses and stay off the streets, that was O.K. We were still a community.'"[15]

God calls some to action, others to support, and still others to pray. Each will be doing what is right in His eyes if they obey His call.

Who's Who:

Ruth and Margaret

CBA radio newsman Charles Osgood once told the story of two elderly ladies—Ruth and Margaret—who lived in a retirement home. Although each was an accomplished pianist, they had both suffered incapacitating strokes. Margaret's stroke paralyzed her left side, and Ruth's stroke permanently damaged her right side. Both women had given up the hope of ever playing the piano again.

Then one day the director of the retirement home had an idea. He sat both Margaret and Ruth down on a piano bench and encouraged them to play one piece together. They did, and a beautiful partnership began!

Like Ruth and Margaret, members of the church have different skills and abilities. But when members combine their strengths and gifts, those partnerships are blessed by God to accomplish much for His Kingdom!

CAUTION: CRITICISM AHEAD!

A DEMANDING WIFE continually nagged her husband to conform to her very high standards: "This is how you should act, this is how you should dress, this is what you should say, this is where you should be seen, and this is how you should plan your career!" She insisted every aspect of his life be honed to perfection. Feeling thoroughly whipped, the man finally said, "Why don't you just write it all down? Then you won't have to tell me these things all the time." She gladly complied.

A short time later the wife died. Within the course of a year, the man met another woman and married. His new life seemed to be a perpetual honeymoon. He could hardly believe the great joy, and relief, he was experiencing with his new bride.

One day he came across the list of "do's and don'ts" his first wife had written. He read them and realized, to his amazement, he was following all of the instructions—even though his second wife had never mentioned them.

He thought about what might have happened and finally said to a friend, "My former wife began her statements, 'I hate it when . . . ,' but my new wife says, 'I just love it when . . .'"

lighten up

There was a young servant girl who worked very hard to please her ultracritical mistress. She always seemed to be most critical at breakfast. If the eggs were scrambled, she complained that they weren't fried. If they were fried, she complained that they were not scrambled.

One morning the girl devised what she thought was a great solution to the problem. She scrambled one egg and fried the other. When she presented them to her mistress, she looked at them and scowled. "This is not right," she said. "You scrambled the wrong one."

When you come across people like this critical mistress, don't take their criticism to heart. Just pray for them and remind yourself that you are completely accepted and loved by your heavenly Father.

"Ninety percent of the **friction** of daily **life** is caused by the wrong tone of voice."

BEING THE AGE YOU ARE

> BIRTHDAYS ARE **GOOD** FOR YOU. STATISTICS SHOW THAT THE **PEOPLE** WHO HAVE THE **MOST** LIVE THE **LONGEST.**
>
> REVEREND LARRY LORENZONI

THERE ONCE was a woman who, upon seeing her hair turn gray, decided she must be getting old. She immediately slowed her pace, refused to wear bright colors, tried to act more sedated, and began to wear "sensible shoes." She let her hair grow long and put it up in a bun on her head, wore long sleeves to cover what she was sure must be unsightly "old lady" arms, and could often be heard telling friends who asked how she was doing, "I suppose I'm doing as well as could be expected for a person my age."

One day she overheard a teenager ask a friend, "How old is Miss Tilly?" The friend said, "Well, from the way she looks and acts, I'd say she's at least 65 or 70." The woman was shocked—they were talking about her, and she was only 55! She decided she was looking far too old for her years and immediately shifted into reverse. Bright colors, high heels, and more stylish clothes rejoined her closet. She cut her hair and used a rinse to color the gray. Several months later, a 48-year-old man asked her out and wouldn't believe her when she told him her age.

She concluded, "Fifty-five is a better speed limit than age limit."

Teach us to **count** our days that
we may gain a **wise** heart.

PSALM 90:12 NRSV

TOP 10 TIPS

for Aging Gracefully

1. WEAR THE COLORS THAT COMPLEMENT YOU.

2. KEEP YOUR MAKEUP SIMPLE.

3. FIND A GOOD HAIRSTYLE AND STICK WITH IT.

4. TAKE CARE OF YOUR TEETH AND KEEP THEM WHITE.

5. GET LOTS OF EXERCISE FOR THAT HEALTHY GLOW.

6. EAT THE RIGHT FOODS TO KEEP YOUR WEIGHT UNDER CONTROL.

7. SPEND TIME WITH FRIENDS WHO MAKE YOU LAUGH.

8. LEARN SOMETHING NEW EVERY DAY.

9. DEDICATE YOURSELF TO A CAUSE LARGER THAN YOU.

10. TRUST IN THE LORD TO BRING YOU THROUGH ALL OF LIFE'S CHANGES.

EACH ONE CAN REACH ONE

When thirteen-year-old Bobby Hill, the son of a U.S. Army sergeant stationed in Italy, read a book about the work of Nobel Prize winner Albert Schweitzer, he decided to do something to help the medical missionary. He sent a bottle of aspirin to Lieutenant General Richard C. Lindsay, Commander of the Allied air forces in Southern Europe, asking if any of his airplanes could parachute the bottle of aspirin to Dr. Schweitzer's jungle hospital in Africa.

Upon hearing the letter, an Italian radio station issued an appeal, resulting in more than $400,000 worth of donated medical supplies. The French and Italian governments each supplied a plane to fly the medicines and the boy to Dr. Schweitzer. The grateful doctor responded, "I never thought a child could do so much for my hospital."

None of us may be able to solve all the problems in the world, but we can feed a hungry family in a nearby neighborhood, clothe the homeless person who has just arrived at a shelter, or give a blanket to a street person who lives near our office building. If every person who could offer help would take just one step every month to meet just one person's need, think what might be accomplished!

> **If you** can't feed a hundred people then just feed one.
>
> MOTHER TERESA

As we have **opportunity**,
let us do **good** to all.

GALATIANS 6:10 NIV

☑ JUST DO IT

#1   Many people don't do anything significant to help others because they feel the need is so great, their small contributions won't matter. But remember the story of the little boy who threw the starfish back into the water? The beach was covered with starfish, **#2** and so a passerby said, "Why bother to do that? There are too many starfish to make a difference. It just doesn't matter."

    The little boy replied, "It mattered to that one."

#3   Maybe you can't contribute to a food pantry every week, but each time you take advantage of a "buy one, get one free" sale on nonperishable goods at the grocery store, you could take the "free one" and set it aside. Soon you'll have quite a supply of goods to **#4** take to a local food pantry. Do so knowing it will make a difference to someone!

#5

#6

#7

#8

HOW Do YOU MEASURE Up?

Shakespeare wrote, "Oh what a tangled web we weave, when first we practice to deceive!" Telling lies, even "white" ones, can become a habit we practice without even realizing it. Check your "web weaving" with this quiz:

1. Your neighbor calls to invite you and your husband over for dinner the following weekend. You want to go, but your husband doesn't. You say:
   A. Sounds like fun! And then call back at the last minute to say your husband is sick.
   B. We're planning to be out of town next weekend.
   C. Sorry, but we have other plans. My husband wants to stay home that night. Maybe another time!

2. Your friend got her hair cut and it looks like the stylist used an egg beater! You say:
   A. Oh, wow! Your hair looks great!
   B. Who did that? I'd love to get mine cut that way.
   C. Nothing.

3. You were behind at work and had to ask a coworker to complete a project for you. The next week your boss compliments you on a job well done. You say:
   A. Thanks. It really went very smoothly.
   B. You're welcome.
   C. Actually, Susie finished it for me. It was a good team effort.

TRUTH OR CONSEQUENCES

THE TROUBLE WITH STRETCHING THE TRUTH IS THAT IT'S APT TO SNAP BACK.

A Sunday school teacher once told her adult class, "Next Sunday I am going to teach a very important lesson. I want you all to read chapter 17 of St. Mark's Gospel in anticipation of it." The members of the class nodded, indicating a willingness to do as the teacher requested.

The following Sunday the teacher asked the class, "Those who read chapter 17 of St. Mark's Gospel during this past week, please raise your hands." Nearly all the people in the room raised their hands.

The teacher then said, "That's very interesting. The Gospel of Mark has only sixteen chapters. But at least I know that my lesson is going to hit its mark. Today I'm going to teach what Jesus had to say about lying."

Perhaps the greatest punishment for lying is not that a person gets caught in the lie, but rather, the "hidden" punishment that a liar can never truly believe what anyone else says.

Tell the truth! You'll suffer far less embarrassment and be much healthier emotionally. Even if truth-telling brings temporary pain, God will honor your courage and bless you for doing the right thing.

A false witness will not go unpunished, and he who speaks lies will not escape.

PROVERBS 19:5 NKJV

CONSIDER THIS!

In a trapeze act, there is a special relationship between the "flyer" and the "catcher." The flyer is the one who must let go, and the catcher is the one who catches him in mid-air. The flyer swings high above the crowd, waiting for the moment when it is time to let go. After letting go, the flyer must be as steady and still as possible, waiting for the strong hands of the catcher to grasp hold of him. The flyer must never try to grab for the catcher. He must wait, suspended in absolute trust that the catcher will be there, at the perfect moment, to save him from falling.

So with us, there are times in life when we must let go and wait. Though we feel that we are suspended in mid-air without any safety net, we must wait, trusting that God will be there at the right time to catch us.

WAITING ON GOD

Several years ago a speedboat driver was in a serious accident. In recounting what had happened, she said that she had been at top speed when her boat veered just slightly, hitting a wave at a dangerous angle. The combined force of her speed and the size and angle of the wave sent the boat spinning wildly into the air. She was thrown from her seat and propelled deeply into the water. She was thrust so deeply into the water that she could not see any light from the surface. Being a little dazed, she had no idea which direction was up.

Rather than panic, the woman remained calm and waited for the buoyancy of her life vest to begin pulling her up. Then she swam heartily in that direction.

EVERYONE HAS PATIENCE. SUCCESSFUL PEOPLE LEARN TO USE IT.

We often find ourselves surrounded by many voices, each with a different opinion, and we simply don't know which way is up. When this happens we need to exercise patience and spend time with the Lord. We must read His Word, the Bible, and wait for His gentle tug on our hearts to pull us toward His will. The more we read, the more confident we will become, especially when His written Word and that gentle tug on our hearts come into agreement.

Remember, a few minutes, hours, days, or even months of "waiting" may mean the difference between sinking or floating.

Let **patience** have its perfect **work**,

that you may be **perfect** and **complete**,

lacking nothing.

JAMES 1:4 NKJV

DON'T PUT IT OFF

WHEN BETH'S BOSS ASKED her to take on an extra project, Beth saw the opportunity to prove she could handle greater responsibility. She immediately began to think how she might approach the task, and her enthusiasm ran high. But when the time came to start the project, Beth found herself telling her boss she was too busy to do the job justice. The project was given to someone else, who earned a promotion for completing it successfully. Beth didn't receive any new opportunities and eventually took a position with another firm.

What had kept Beth from doing the project? Simple procrastination. She put off getting started on the project until she was paralyzed with fear— fear that she might not be able to do the job or that her performance would not meet her boss' expectation. In the end, Beth didn't move ahead and thus reinforced her fears with a bigger sense of insecurity about her own ability.

If you find yourself procrastinating, ask God to show you how to overcome your fear, then do what He says. He wants you to succeed and live a fulfilled life, but you must step out in faith for Him to bless you.

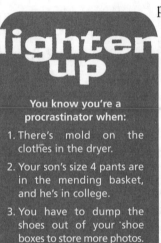

lighten up

You know you're a procrastinator when:

1. There's mold on the clothes in the dryer.

2. Your son's size 4 pants are in the mending basket, and he's in college.

3. You have to dump the shoes out of your 'shoe boxes to store more photos.

4. The first chapter of that novel you're going to finish was typed on an electric typewriter.

5. The oil in your car is so dense it won't drain out.

6. You find last year's unsent Christmas cards under the bed during spring cleaning.

Joshua said to the Israelites, "How long will you of the land that the Lord, the God of your

"If you want to make an easy job seem hard, just keep putting off doing it."

be slack about going in and taking possession ancestors, has given you?" JOSHUA 18:3 NRSV

KEEP YOUR
WORDS POSITIVE

It takes just as much energy to say a positive word as it does a negative one. In fact, it may take even less. Research has shown that when we speak positive words—even in difficult circumstances or troubling situations—our bodies relax. As we relax, blood flow increases, including the flow of blood to the brain. A well-oxygenated brain is much more likely to think creatively, make wise decisions, find reasonable solutions, and generate answers to questions.

Positive words ease relationships and create an atmosphere of peace that is conducive to rest, relaxation, rejuvenation, and sleep—all of which are necessary for good health.

On the other hand, contrary to popular thought, negative words do not release tension. They keep the body in a state of tension, constricting muscles and blood vessels. Irrational, uncreative, unreasonable behavior is a secondary effect.

A continual flow of negative words causes relationships to suffer, which creates an atmosphere of disharmony and makes for fitful sleep and frayed nerves—none of which are healthy.

One of the best things we can do for our overall health is to transform our speech habits.

> GOOD WORDS ARE WORTH MUCH, AND COST LITTLE.
>
> WILLIAM FEATHER

PLEASANT WORDS ARE A HONEYCOMB,
SWEET TO THE SOUL
AND HEALING TO THE BONES.

PROVERBS 16:24 NASB

WISE WORDS

Words are not just letters strung together. Words
are the incarnation of emotions and the stimula-
tors of emotion. A word can be a balm or a
bomb. A positive word makes you feel good. A
negative word leaves you feeling depressed and
defeated. Words release energy. A single word
can turn you on, or it can turn you off. A negative word can defuse your enthusiasm for a project. A positive word releases positive energy
and becomes a creative force.

ROBERT SCHULLER

"The only way to have a
FRIEND
is to be one."

RALPH WALDO EMERSON

BE A FRIEND

A young family in the 1950s had just purchased their first television set. All the neighbors gathered to help them put up the antenna on the roof of their home. Since they had only the simplest of tools, they weren't making much progress.

Then a new neighbor and his wife showed up with a large, elaborate toolbox, filled with just about any gadget or tool one could imagine. They had everything needed to install the antenna, which was up in near record time after their arrival.

The group of volunteers immediately went inside to see what kind of reception their neighbors would get on their new television set. The picture was crystal clear! Success was theirs!

As the neighbors stood around congratulating themselves on their fine work, they thanked their new neighbors for their valuable assistance. One of the women asked, "What is it that you make with such a well-equipped toolbox?"

The new neighbors smiled sincerely and replied with genuine warmth, "Friends."

Who's Who:

Thomas Hughes

The lesson of friendship we were taught as children serves us throughout our lives: To have a friend, be a friend. So often, the bridge to friendship is crossed when one person reaches out to share that which he or she has with another. Author Thomas Hughes, who lived from 1822-1896, had this to say about the art of friendship:

"Blessed are they who have the gift of making friends, for it is one of God's best gifts. It involves many things, but above all, the power of going out of one's self, and appreciating whatever is noble and loving in another."

LIGHTEN SOMEONE'S BURDEN

Carol Porter, a registered nurse, is a co-founder of Kid-Care, Inc., a nonprofit group with a volunteer staff who deliver five hundred free meals each day to poor neighborhoods. Each meal is prepared in Porter's cramped Houston home, where extra stoves and refrigerators have been installed in what used to be the family's living room and den. Kid-Care receives no public funding, and although Carol's efforts have resulted in help from some corporations, most of her $500,000 budget comes from individual donations.

> **No one is** useless in this world who lightens the burden of it to anyone else.
>
> CHARLES DICKENS

Carol credits her late mother, Lula Doe, for giving her the idea for Kid-Care. In 1984 Lula persuaded a local supermarket not to discard its blemished produce, but to let her distribute it to the poor.

During Christmastime in 1989, Carol saw a group of children searching for food in a McDonalds' dumpster. She says, "I saw Third World conditions a stone's throw from where I live." Kid-Care was her response.

"People ask me what's in it for me. And I tell them to go the route with me and see my kids' faces. That's what's in it for me." She sees the meals as "better than ice cream. . . . It's hope."[15]

Purpose in life comes when we purpose to lift the load of another—to show God's love by doing for them what they could not do for themselves.

Bear ye one another's **burdens,** and so **fulfil** the law of **Christ.**

GALATIANS 6:2 KJV

#1   The phrase "one another" is a popular one in the New Testament, appearing 59 times! Look up the following verses in the New International Version to fill in the blanks. Then think about the relationships in your life. Do you treat people according to these "one another" verses?

- A new command I give you: _____ one another. John 13:34
- Be _____ to one another in brotherly love. _____ one another above yourselves. Romans 12:10
- Therefore let us stop passing _____ on one another. Romans 14:13
- Be _____, bearing with one another in love. Ephesians 4:2
- _____ one another daily, as long as it is called Today. Hebrews 3:13
- Offer _____ to one another without grumbling. 1 Peter 4:9
- Clothe yourselves with _____ toward one another. 1 Peter 5:5

SEEING OTHERS THROUGH LOVE

HAVE YOU EVER NOTICED:

When others are set in their ways, they're obstinate, but you are firm and resolved.

When your neighbor doesn't like your friend, she's prejudiced, but when you don't like her friend, you're a good judge of human nature.

When she tries to treat someone especially well, she's buttering up the person, but when you do so, you're being thoughtful.

When she takes time to do things well, she's lazy, but when you do so, you're meticulous.

When she spends a lot, she's a spendthrift, but when you overdo, you're generous.

When she picks flaws in things, she's critical, but when you do, you are perceptive.

When she is mild-mannered, you call her weak, but when you are, you're gracious.

When she dresses well, she is extravagant, but when you do, you're tastefully in style.

When she says what she thinks, she's spiteful, but when you do, you're being honest.

When she takes great risks, she's foolhardy, but when you do, you're brave.

> **Faults** are thick where love is thin.
> JAMES HOWELL

Above all things have fervent love for one another, for "love will cover a multitude of sins."

1 PETER 4:8 NKJV

new insights into ageless questions

I want to see the best in people, but it seems like the harder I try the more their faults seem to stick out like sore thumbs. When I first meet someone, I tend to like them a lot, but then I notice irritating things about them. Why can't I focus on the good in people?

It's human nature to notice the things you don't like in others while perhaps being blind to the same shortcomings in yourself. We all do it, even if we aren't all honest enough to admit it. As Christians, however, we have been given a way out of those behaviors we want to change. In fact, they have no power over us at all, if we are willing to submit them to God and learn a better way. That will take solid commitment and a willingness to submit to the authority of the Holy Spirit in your life.

Why don't you start with prayer. Ask God to help you break the habit of being overly critical by doing what Mother Teresa told the sisters who worked with her to do, which was to "see Jesus Christ in every face." And when you look at people the way Jesus does, you will find them much easier to love.

Trivia

Fun

The century plant, a common sight in the Southwest, has an interesting growth cycle. For 20 or 30 years the plant will remain the same height. Then, suddenly, a bud will sprout. The bud will shoot straight up into the sky, like a giant asparagus spear, at the amazing rate of seven inches per day. It will eventually reach a height of 20 to 40 feet, crowning itself with clumps of beautiful yellow blossoms.

Like the century plant, great things in our lives often happen only after years of patience and behind-the-scenes preparation.

PATIENCE PAYS OFF

Diligence is the mother
of good **fortune.**

CERVANTES

On a shelf sits a beautiful and expensive carving from the Orient. It is a statue of a lady wearing a tall headdress, and balanced atop the headdress is an intricately carved ball. Inside that seamless sphere is another slightly smaller sphere of equal intricacy—and inside that still another, and then another—until one can no longer see through the tiny carved holes to see how many more balls there actually are.

Several things make this orb truly remarkable. Each of the nested balls is seamless, completely free from the one outside it and inside it, and magnificent in its airy, lacy design. The orb was carved from a single piece of ivory over one hundred years ago, before the days of electronic magnifying instruments.

Why did the artist carve so many layers with such precision? The smallest orbs would not be clearly seen by most people, yet each one was finished with as much skill and artistry as was applied to the larger, outer ones.

The small details of a job may not always remain unnoticed or unseen. Like this artist, your excellence in small things can bring you prosperity in this life and make you a legend for future generations to follow.

The hand of the **diligent**
makes [one] **rich.**

PROVERBS 10:4 NKJV

booklist

BE HONEST BUT WISE

THE EDITOR OF THE "weddings and engagement" section of a small-town newspaper grew tired of hearing from the town's citizens that she always embellished her reports of parties and celebrations. She decided that in the next issue she was going to tell the truth and see if she had greater favor with the citizenry. She wrote the following item:

"Married—Miss Sylvan Rhodes and James Collins, last Saturday at the Baptist parsonage, by the Rev. J. Gordon. The bride is a very ordinary town girl, who doesn't know any more about cooking than a jackrabbit and never helped her mother three days in her life. She is not a beauty by any means and has a gait like a duck. The groom is an up-to-date loafer. He has been living off the old folks at home all his life and is now worth shucks. It will be a hard life."

We may not always need to be so brutally "honest" in telling the truth! Truth, after all, is ultimately known only by God—who alone has the ability to see into the hearts of men and women and know everything involved in any situation or relationship. Rather, we should be honest in expressing our hopes for another person's best welfare and success. That is a truth everybody loves to hear.

> **Honesty** is the first chapter of the book of wisdom.
> THOMAS JEFFERSON

Provide things **honest** in the **sight** of all **men.**

ROMANS 12:17 KJV

THE LIGHT OF VIRTUE

Herbert V. Prochnow has constructed a ten-part "Character Quiz"—an interesting checkup as to just how much we might choose to be "children of light":

1. If you found a wallet with $1,000, would you give it to the owner if no one knew you found it?
2. If you could advance yourself unfairly, would you do it if no one would ever find out?
3. If the bus driver failed to collect your fare, would you voluntarily pay it?
4. If there were no locks on any house, store, or bank, would you take anything if no one found out?
5. If your business partner died, would you pay his relatives their fair share, if you didn't have to?
6. If you are an employer, would you hire yourself at your salary?
7. If you are an employer, would you like to be working for yourself?
8. If you are a parent, would you like to be the child of a parent like you?
9. If you had a choice, would you like to live in a community with people working in church, civic, and community affairs like you do?
10. If you had to live with someone just like you for the rest of your life, would you count it a privilege?[16]

> **Do not in** the darkness of night what you'd shun in broad daylight.

THE NIGHT IS FAR SPENT, THE DAY IS AT HAND: LET US THEREFORE CAST OFF THE WORKS OF DARKNESS, AND LET US PUT ON THE ARMOUR OF LIGHT.

ROMANS 13:12 KJV

WISE WORDS

Whenever we have a choice between doing what is right and honorable and doing something less than that for our own gain, our personal virtue comes into play. As Christians, we rely on the Holy Spirit to speak to us about the choices we make, trusting that He will always lead us to make the choices Jesus would make. Only then can we be consistently virtuous! John Stuart Mill (1806-1873) explains it this way: "It would not be easy, even for an unbeliever, to find a better translation of the rule of virtue from the abstract into the concrete, than to endeavor so to live that Christ would approve our life."

AVOID THE BLAME GAME

EVERY **JOB** IS A **SELF-PORTRAIT** OF THE PERSON WHO DOES IT. **AUTOGRAPH** YOUR WORK WITH **EXCELLENCE.**

SOMEONE ONCE asked Al Jolson, a popular musical comedy star of the twenties, what he did to warm up a cold audience. Jolson answered, "Whenever I go out before an audience and don't get the response I feel that I ought to get, . . . I don't go back behind the scenes and say to myself, 'That audience is dead from the neck up—it's a bunch of wooden nutmegs.' No, instead I say to myself, 'Look here, Al, what is wrong with you tonight? The audience is all right, but you're all wrong, Al.'"

Many a performer has blamed a poor showing on an audience. Al Jolson took a different approach. He tried to give the best performance of his career to his coldest, most unresponsive audiences, and the result was that before an evening was over, he had them applauding and begging for more.

You'll always be able to find excuses for mediocrity. In fact, a person intent on justifying a bad performance usually has excuses lined up before the final curtain falls. Choose instead to put your full energy into your performance. Your extra effort will turn an average performance into something outstanding.

Ah, the joys of a job well done. That is true satisfaction!

Many **daughters** have done **well,** but you **excel** them all.

PROVERBS 31:29 NKJV

TOP 10 EXCUSES

Many Employers Hear

Business consultant James M. Bleech of Jacksonville, Florida, surveyed 110 executives to find out what excuses they hear most from their employees. Here are the top 10:

1. IT'S NOT MY FAULT.
2. IT WAS SOMEONE ELSE'S FAULT.
3. SOMETHING ELSE CAME UP.
4. I DIDN'T HAVE TIME.
5. WE'VE NEVER DONE IT THAT WAY BEFORE.
6. NO ONE TOLD ME TO DO IT.
7. I HAD TOO MANY INTERRUPTIONS.
8. IF ONLY MY SUPERVISOR REALLY UNDERSTOOD...
9. I WILL GET TO IT LATER.
10. NO ONE SHOWED ME HOW TO DO IT.

These excuses don't impress employers—and they certainly don't impress God! Make it your goal to live a life without excuses.

"Expect great things FROM God. Attempt great things for God."

WILLIAM CAREY

KINGDOM GREATNESS

Gladys Aylward saw herself as a simple woman who just did what God called her to do. Yet, her life was so remarkable that both a book (*The Small Woman*) and a movie (*The Inn of the Sixth Happiness*) were produced about the great things God accomplished through her.

A British citizen, Aylward left her home in 1920 and sailed for China. There she bought orphans who were being systematically discarded, children who had been displaced by the political upheavals of the time and left to starve or wander on their own until placed in government warehouses. Gladys gave these children a home.

When the Japanese invaded China, she was forced to flee the mainland with one hundred children. She ended up on the island of Formosa with her charges. There she continued to devote her life to raising children who knew no other mother.

Gladys explains her amazing work for God like this: "I did not choose this. I was led into it by God. I am not really more interested in children than I am in other people, but God through His Holy Spirit gave me to understand that this is what He wanted me to do, so I did."

Who's Who:

Oseola McCarty

Until 1995, Oseola McCarty lived in obscurity in Hattiesburg, Mississippi. In the sixth grade, she dropped out of school to help care for an ailing family member and help her mother with the laundry. Later, she began to do laundry for people in Hattiesburg for fifty cents a load. A thrifty person and devout Christian, Oseola used her meager income to pay her bills each week. Then she deposited whatever was left over into a savings account.

Finally, when she was eighty-six years old, a banker sat down with Oseola to talk to her about what she wanted done with the money in her savings account if she should die. He revealed, to her astonishment, that she had a quarter of a million dollars in the bank!

She decided to quietly donate $150,000 to a scholarship fund at the University of Southern Mississippi, to give other African Americans something she never had: the opportunity to get a college education.

When word got out about Oseola and her gift, the old woman was an instant celebrity, appearing on several TV talk shows and even receiving an honorary doctorate of humane letters from Harvard University.

Like Oseola, each of us has the capacity to be great in God's Kingdom. All we have to do is be willing to give ourselves away!

USE YOUR TIME WISELY

A woman once had a dream that an angel was giving her this message: "As a reward for your virtues, the sum of $1,440 will be deposited into your bank account every morning. This amount has only one condition. At the close of each business day, any balance that has not been used will be canceled. It won't carry over to the next day or accrue interest. Each morning, a new $1,440 will be credited to you."

The dream was so vivid, she asked the Lord to show her what it meant. He led her to realize she was receiving 1,440 minutes every morning, the total number of minutes in a 24-hour day. What she did with this deposit of time was important, because 1,440 minutes per day was all she would ever receive!

Each of us has a similar account. At the close of each "business" day, we should be able to look over our ledger and see that these golden minutes were spent wisely.

Time is God's gift to you. What you do with your time is your gift to God.

> **Remember** how short my time is.
> PSALM 89:47 NRSV

"Dost thou love life?
Then do not squander time, for that is the stuff life is made of."

BENJAMIN FRANKLIN

☑ JUST DO IT

Our lives are so filled with "busy-ness," we often fail to take the time to just stop and appreciate God's everyday gifts to us. Take a few minutes and make a list of the things you most enjoy experiencing through your five senses—touch, taste, hearing, sight, and smell. Below are a few examples to get you started. After you've come up with your list, thank God for these special blessings—and don't forget to take the time to enjoy them!

Touch
- A child's hand in yours
- A puppy licking your face
- Beach sand between your toes

Taste
- A rich, dark chocolate truffle
- Cold lemonade on a hot day
- A freshly picked raspberry

Hearing
- A mother talking to her newborn baby
- The scrunch of autumn leaves
- A stadium crowd singing the national anthem

Sight
- A double rainbow
- A friend arriving at the airport
- Someone else doing the dishes

Smell
- Newly mowed grass
- An apple pie baking
- Laundry fresh from

CONSIDER
THIS!

It might seem odd, but one of the best things a farmer can do to his fields to make them thrive is to start a fire. A burned field looks completely barren, like it could never support another shred of life. But fire actually stimulates the growth of new plants by returning vital nutrients to the soil and exposing the land to sunlight.

Just like setting a fire to stimulate growth in a field, the way God works in our lives often doesn't make sense to our mortal minds. God doesn't bring adverse circumstances into our lives, but He does use them to cleanse and renew us if we will let Him. It is the principle that was set in place when His ravaged and broken body was laid to rest in a borrowed tomb. When all seemed lost, God called Him forth to be the firstfruits of resurrection power. New growth from ashes. New life from the curse of death, You can always be sure that whatever happens, God is working to make you thrive!

GOD'S MYSTERIOUS WAYS

Bernard Gilpin was accused of heresy before Bishop Bonner, and shortly thereafter was sent to London for trial. Gilpin's favorite saying was, "All things are for the best." He set out on his journey with that attitude, but on his way fell from his horse and broke his leg.

> IT IS GOOD TO REMEMBER THAT THE TEA KETTLE, ALTHOUGH UP TO ITS NECK IN HOT WATER, CONTINUES TO SING.

"Is all for the best now?" a scorner said, mocking Gilpin for his optimism. "I still believe so," he replied.

He turned out to be right. During the time he was convalescing from the accident, and before he was able to resume his journey, Queen Mary died. Consequently, the case against him was dropped. Instead of being burned at the stake, Gilpin returned home in triumph.

We tend to see all accidents and illness that come our way as misfortune caused by the enemy of our souls. That may not always be the case. Rather than spend our energy railing against bad times, perhaps we should direct our effort toward praising the One who promises to work all things together for the good of those who are called according to His purposes. (See Romans 8:28.) God has many methods and means for accomplishing His plan!

Rejoice evermore. . . . In every thing give thanks: for this is the will of God in Christ Jesus concerning you.

1 THESSALONIANS 5:16,18 KJV

HOW Do YOU MEASURE Up?

Take this quiz to see how your contentment measures up.

1. When a friend buys a cute new pair of shoes, I:
   - A. Pay her a sincere compliment.
   - B. Pretend not to notice.
   - C. Buy a more expensive pair than hers.

2. When I'm at the mall, I:
   - A. Avoid the temptation to buy things I don't really need.
   - B. Charge things I can't afford because "I deserve them."
   - C. Buy two of everything . . . just in case.

3. When I look around my house, I:
   - A. Thank God for everything He's blessed me with.
   - B. Mentally replace all my furnishings with newer items.
   - C. Wish I could clear everything out and start over.

BE CONTENT

THE GRASS MAY BE GREENER ON THE OTHER SIDE, BUT IT STILL HAS TO BE MOWED.

Several years ago, a newspaper cartoon was drawn of two fields divided by a fence. Both were about the same size, and each had plenty of lush, green grass.

Each field had a mule whose head stuck through the wire fence, eating grass from the other's pasture. The neighboring field seemed somewhat more desirable—even though it was harder to reach.

In the process, the mules' heads became caught in the fence. They panicked and brayed uncontrollably at being unable to free themselves. The cartoonist wisely described the situation with one caption: "DISCONTENT."

Like the mules, when we focus on what we don't have we become blinded to the blessings which surround us. There is nothing wrong with desiring something, but to think life is easier in someone else's pasture may not be true. Besides, no matter whose pasture we are in, we will always have to deal with the attitudes of our own heart.

If there is something you desire in life, perhaps a home, a better car, or even your own business, look to Jesus to help you bring it to pass. And while He is working on it, remember to find pleasure in what He's already given you!

Be **content** with such **things** as you **have**.

HEBREWS 13:5 NKJV

THE IMPORTANCE OF COMMUNITY

The next time you visit a very dense forest, try to imagine what is taking place under your feet. Scientists now know when the roots of trees come into contact with one another, a substance is released which encourages the growth of a particular kind of fungus. This fungus helps link roots of different trees—even those of dissimilar species. If one tree has access to water, another to nutrients, and a third to sunlight, the fungus enables the transfer of these items to trees that may be in need. Thus the trees have the means of sharing with one another to preserve them all.

Our culture today applauds individualism. This isolates people from one another and cuts them off from the mainstream of life. With more and more people working at home or in walled offices, and with schedules crammed tighter than ever with work and activities, feelings of loneliness are more likely to increase than decrease. Don't allow isolation to overcome you!

Reach out to others. Begin to give where you can. Learn to receive when others give to you. Build a network of friends, not just colleagues. And above all, root yourself in a group that nourishes you spiritually—a church.

REMEMBER THE BANANA— WHEN IT LEFT THE BUNCH, IT GOT SKINNED.

NOT FORSAKING THE ASSEMBLING OF OURSELVES TOGETHER, AS THE MANNER OF SOME IS; BUT EXHORTING ONE ANOTHER; AND SO MUCH THE MORE, AS YE SEE THE DAY APPROACHING.

HEBREWS 10:25 KJV

WISE WORDS

One thing about the New Testament church. There's a climate of loving relationships. A sense of warmth and care permeates the whole, and fondness for individuals breaks through repeatedly. People know how to love and be loved by each other.

NORM WAKEFIELD

Trivia

Americans love Mexican food. In fact, the Mexican food craze mushroomed in the '90s, becoming a $1.6 billion industry by 1996. Originally, the market started with small companies like El Paso Chile in Texas which stayed true to the cuisine's spicy roots. When larger food companies like Pillsbury saw the potential in marketing Mexican-style food, they changed the original cuisine to suit the tastes of most Americans, producing what experts call "gringo food."

In a *New York Times* article, Dr. Benadette Paicek-Llanes of Pillsbury's specialty brands, including Old El Paso, said, "Forty percent of those on the East Coast want salsa as mild as it can be." In fact, Bob Messenger, editor of the industry publication *Food Processing,* says that the "gringo-ization of Mexican food will continue. In 20 years, you won't even recognize what they'll be calling Mexican food."

Although it is legitimate in the industry to make ethnic foods more palatable for other cultures, the same sort of thing sometimes happens in the Christian life. To please as many people as possible, we are tempted to water down our witness. We must consistently be on guard against this temptation, keeping in mind that our obligation is to please God—not people!

IT'S PLEASING GOD THAT MATTERS

I don't know the **secret** to
success, but the **key** to **failure**
is to **try** to please everyone.

BILL COSBY

The story is told of a painter who desired to produce one work which would please the entire world. She drew a picture which required her utmost skill and took it to the public marketplace. She posted directions at the bottom of the piece for spectators to mark with a brush each portion of the picture that didn't meet their approval. The spectators came and, in general, applauded the work. But each, eager to make a personal critique, marked a small portion of the picture. By evening, the painter was mortified to find the entire picture had become a blot.

The next day the painter returned with a copy of the first picture. This time she asked the spectators to mark the portions of the work they admired. The spectators again complied. When the artist returned several hours later, she found every stroke that had been panned the day before had received praise by this day's critics.

The artist concluded, "I now believe the best way to please one-half of the world is not to mind what the other says."

People will always have an opinion about what we say or do. That is why we live our lives according to the words of the Bible—God's opinion. Then we will not fret over the opinions of others.

Jesus said, "No one can **serve two** masters;
for either he will **hate** the one and **love** the other,
or he will be devoted to one and despise the other."

MATTHEW 6:24 NASB

REACTING GOD'S WAY

THE MOTHER OF SIX children walked into her house one day to see all her children huddled together in a circle. She approached them to see what had evoked such intense interest, and she could hardly believe her eyes.

To her horror, in the middle of the circle of children were several baby skunks. She immediately screamed at the top of her voice, "Children! Run, run, run! Out, out, out!"

At the sound of their mother's alarmed voice, each child quickly grabbed a baby skunk and headed for the door. The screaming and panic, of course, set off the instinctual danger alarm in the skunks, and each of them quickly dispelled its horrible scent. Each child and the house itself were doused with an aroma that lingered for weeks, regardless of intense scrubbing and use of disinfectants.

How we react has greater negative consequences than the initial negative situation we encounter! Don't make matters worse by unplanned, emotion-driven, spur-of-the-moment behavior. Choose to act rather than to react, taking sufficient time to select a course of action based upon calm reason and thoughtful prayer.

> **Hindsight explains the injury that foresight would have prevented.**

Do not forsake **wisdom,** and she will **protect** you. . . . When you walk, your **steps** will not be hampered; when you **run,** you will not **stumble.**

PROVERBS 4:6,12 NIV

new insights into ageless questions

I work outside the home, and our family runs on a tight schedule. I seem to be able to stay fairly calm as long as things are going smoothly, but when a child is too sick to go to school or the car breaks down, I always seem to overreact. This just makes things worse. How can I handle unexpected events more calmly?

It's possible that your schedule, and your life, are so tightly programmed that there simply isn't any room for deviation. First of all, ask yourself what could be eliminated on a permanent basis. Could you cut back on your work hours or work closer to home to shorten your commute time? Could you set up a "back-up plan" with a neighbor that would be mutually beneficial? Second, ask the Lord to help you keep such events in perspective. Your child is sick, but it's probably not life threatening. Your car won't start, but you do have a car. Be grateful for the part of your day that can be salvaged, and ask God to give you the patience and the wisdom to handle the unexpected.

THE COURAGE TO LEAD

MANY YEARS AGO AN intern in a New York hospital heard a surgeon bemoan the fact that most brain tumors are fatal. The surgeon predicted someday a surgeon would discover how to save the lives of these patients. Intern Ernest Sachs dared to be that surgeon. At the time, the leading expert on the anatomy of the brain was Sir Victor Horsley. Sachs received permission to study under him, but felt he should prepare for the experience by studying for six months under some of the most able physicians in Germany. Then he went to England, where for two years he assisted Dr. Horsley in long and intricate experiments on dozens of monkeys.

When Sachs returned to America, he was ridiculed for requesting the opportunity to treat brain tumors. For years he fought obstacles and discouragement, driven by an uncontrollable urge to succeed in his quest. Today, largely thanks to Dr. Sachs, the majority of brain tumors can be cured. His book, *The Diagnosis and Treatment of Brain Tumors,* is considered the standard authority on the subject.

Because something isn't presently done doesn't mean it can't be done. And maybe you are the one to do it!

lighten up

There once was a group of tourists visiting a small, picturesque town. On their tour of the town, they passed by an old man sitting on a park bench. One of the tourists asked the old man, "Were any great men born in this town?" Without hesitation, the old man said, "Nope, only babies."

In fact, there is no such thing as an "instant leader." True leaders in life emerge over time, as they doggedly pursue a cause, never giving up or allowing themselves to be deterred by obstacles. Is God calling you to be a leader? Then go for it, with the confidence that He will give you the determination, courage, and resources to succeed!

> **Do not follow** where the **path** may lead—go **instead** where there is no path and **leave** a trail.

"**This is the way, walk in it.**" ISAIAH 30:21 NKJV

WASHING AWAY OLD MISTAKES

When Cathy met Jim at a softball game, she thought he was the man for her—everything she was looking for! After several months of dating, Cathy was as sold on Jim as ever, except it bothered her that he found so many excuses for drinking alcohol. "I got a raise!" "My friend is getting married!" "My sister is graduating from college!"

Despite her friends' warnings and her own misgivings, Cathy married Jim. Before long, however, the marriage was destroyed by Jim's drinking. When the divorce was final, Cathy felt destroyed too. By ignoring the Holy Spirit's warning and her friends' wise counsel, she had made one of the biggest mistakes a Christian could make. I wanted to have my way instead of God's," Cathy told her pastor. "I thought I knew what was best for me."

> **Decisions** can take you out of God's will but never out of His reach.

"We all think that sometimes," Cathy's pastor said. "We forget that the One who created us knows us better than we know ourselves. But remember, Cathy, He never gives up on us! When we admit our mistakes, He always forgives us and gives us another chance."

Recovering from the bad choices we've made can be heartwrenching and difficult, but God is always right there ready to make us whole and give us a brand new life.

If we are faithless, he will remain faithful, for he cannot disown himself.

2 TIMOTHY 2:13 NIV

#1   Baptism is a beautiful symbol of God's washing away our sins and making us clean and pure in His sight. The next time you are convicted by the Holy Spirit of a sin in your life, and you repent of that sin, use the symbolism of baptism to "wash" the sin out of your mind and heart. While you are in the shower or bath, scoop some water into your hands and pour it over your head. Say a prayer as you do so, thanking God for loving you and for forgiving your sin, forever washing it away. This symbolic practice will help you release the feelings of guilt that Satan often uses to torment us, even after God has extended His complete forgiveness.

#2

#3

#4

#5

#6

#7

#8

#9

#10

"The world wants your **BEST** but God wants your all."

CHARLES H. SPURGEON

WORK AS FOR THE LORD

Janette Oke, best-selling novelist with more than forty books to her credit, is considered the modern "pioneer author" for Christian fiction. Her books have sold millions of copies since her first novel was published in 1979.

When she first decided to write, she said to God, "Lord, I'm going to write this book. If it works, and if I discover I have talent, I'll give it all to You."

Janette sensed God was not pleased with the bargain she was trying to strike with Him. She felt in her heart as if He were responding, "If you're serious about this, then I want everything before you start." Thus she gave Him her ambitions and dreams, and trusted Him to teach her, whether she was successful or not. Out of that resolve came a second resolve. She refused to compromise her principles. Although she would write realistically, her stories would be "wholesome and good and encouraging." Many thought that approach was doomed to failure at the outset, but a shelf of novels later . . . Janette Oke has proven "God can teach spiritual truths through fictional characters."[17]

Who's Who:

The Proverbs 31 Woman

God clearly asks for nothing but the best we have to offer. The woman described in Proverbs 31 is clearly such an example for women. Her excellence is not presented to make us feel inadequate, but rather to present the full range of opportunity available to women willing to work as for the Lord.

She supports her husband in many ways, and he is proud of her. She makes wise purchases to provide for her family and sews their clothes from fine fabrics. She develops a business to bring in some extra income. She makes her home a beacon of hospitality, reaching out to the needy and keeping her lamp glowing all night as a sign to travelers that they are welcome. And she does it all with a sense of humor and a great deal of wisdom!

God doesn't expect us to do all these things at the same time. Rather our lives are made up of seasons. But eventually we too, by relying on Him, can live a life characterized by excellence.

LEARNING IS FOREVER

> LET THE **WISE** ALSO HEAR AND **GAIN** IN **LEARNING**, AND THE **DISCERNING** ACQUIRE **SKILL**.
>
> PROVERBS 1:5 NRSV

CARLOS ROMULO, the former president of the Philippines, won an oratorical contest in the Manila high school he attended as a young man. His father was puzzled, however, when he saw his son ignore the congratulations of one of the other contestants. As they left the auditorium he asked, "Why didn't you shake hands with Julio?"

Carlos said, "I have no use for Julio. He was speaking ill of me before the contest." The father put his arm around his son and said, "Your grandfather used to tell me that the taller the bamboo grows, the lower it bends. Remember that always, my boy. The taller the bamboo grows, the lower it bends."

Every person has something to teach us—not only those who are experts in their fields or tell us what we want to hear. Each person is a living encyclopedia of ideas, insights, facts, experiences, and opinions.

A woman once advised a new employee: "Fifty percent of the people in this organization will teach you what to do and the other 50 percent what not to do. It's your challenge to figure out which percent goes with which person." Even if a person doesn't have a good example for you to follow, you can always learn from him or her what not to do!

I am defeated, and know it, if I meet any human being from whom I find myself unable to learn anything.

GEORGE HERBERT PALMER

TOP 10 TIPS

for Learning Something New Every Day

1. WATCH AN EDUCATIONAL TV PROGRAM ON A SUBJECT YOU KNOW LITTLE ABOUT.

2. OPEN THE DICTIONARY AND LEARN A NEW WORD. USE IT THREE TIMES IN ONE DAY.

3. REALLY LISTEN TO AN OPINION THAT DIFFERS FROM YOURS.

4. USING A STUDY BIBLE, READ ALL THE NOTES FOR A PASSAGE OF SCRIPTURE.

5. ASK A SMALL CHILD TO DEFINE LOVE, SHARING, OR FRIENDSHIP.

6. ATTEND A FREE LECTURE AT A LOCAL UNIVERSITY OR COMMUNITY COLLEGE.

7. VISIT A MUSEUM OR FINE ARTS CENTER AND TAKE THE GUIDED TOUR.

8. ASK SOMEONE 75 OR OLDER WHAT HIS OR HER LIFE WAS LIKE AS A CHILD.

9. ASK YOUR SPOUSE OR A CLOSE FRIEND WHAT THEY SEE AS YOUR 5 STRENGTHS—AND 5 WEAKNESSES.

10. BEGIN THE DAY BY ASKING THE LORD TO "OPEN THE EYES OF YOUR HEART."

LET CONSCIENCE RULE

In the 1890s a man drove by the farm of Mrs. John R. McDonald. A sudden gust of wind caught his black derby hat and whirled it onto the McDonald property. He searched in vain for the hat and finally drove off bareheaded.

Mrs. McDonald retrieved the hat, and for the next forty-five years various members of her family wore it. Finally the old derby was beyond repair, completely worn out. It was at that point Mrs. McDonald went to the local newspaper and advertised for the owner of the hat. She noted in her ad that while the hat had been on the heads of the menfolk in her family, the hat had been on her conscience for forty-five years!

> A LOT OF PEOPLE MISTAKE A SHORT MEMORY FOR A CLEAR CONSCIENCE.
>
> DOUG LARSEN

Is something nagging at your heart today—an awareness that you have committed a wrong against another person or a feeling that something has gone amiss in a relationship? Don't "stuff" those feelings. Seek to make amends. The sooner you do, the easier you'll find the reconciliation of restoration—and the easier you'll find your rest at night.

A guilty conscience is a very heavy load to carry through life—one for which Jesus died on the cross. He did His part. Now you do yours and obtain the freedom and peace He purchased for you!

I DO MY LEVEL BEST TO KEEP A CLEAR CONSCIENCE BEFORE GOD AND MY NEIGHBORS IN EVERYTHING I DO.

ACTS 24:16 MSG

WISE WORDS

Conscience is that faculty in me which attaches itself to the highest that I know, and tells me what the highest I know demands that I do. It is the eye of the soul which looks out either towards God or towards what it regards as the highest, and therefore conscience records differently in different people. If I am in the habit of steadily facing myself with God, my conscience will always introduce God's perfect law and indicate what I should do. The point is, will I obey? I have to make an effort to keep my conscience so sensitive that I walk without offence.

OSWALD CHAMBERS

booklist

read more about it...acceptance and forgiveness

- *Forgive and Forget: Healing the Hurts We Don't Deserve*
  by Lewis B. Smedes

- *Love, Acceptance & Forgiveness*
  by Stanley Baldwin

- *Freedom through Forgiveness*
  by Charles Stanley

- *The Prayer of Revenge*
  by Doug Schmidt

- *Forgiveness*
  by John Arnott,

- *Total Forgiveness*
  by R. T. Kendall

- *Embracing Forgiveness*
  by Traci Mullins

ACCEPTING OTHERS NO MATTER WHAT

IN *LEARNING TO FORGIVE,* Doris Donnelly writes, "Some years ago I met a family very proficient in the use of scissors. . . . The friends of each family member were under constant scrutiny to determine whether they measured up to the standards imposed by mother and father. One slip . . . resulted in ostracism from the narrow circle of 'friends.' . . . Anyone who did not respond immediately with profuse gratitude was eliminated from the list for the next time. Snip.

"Eventually I, too, was scissored out of their lives. I never knew for sure why, but I knew enough to recognize that once I was snipped away there was no hope of my being sewn into their lives again.

The Bridge you burn now may be the one you later have to cross.

"Last year the mother of the family died. The father and daughters, expecting large crowds to gather to say their final farewells, enlisted the assistance of the local police to handle traffic. . . . Telegrams were sent . . . phone calls were made . . . local motels were alerted . . . yet in the end, only the husband, the daughters, their husbands, and a grandchild or two attended the services."[18]

Cutting imperfect people out of our lives is a prescription for loneliness. Who would remain to be our friends? Is there anyone you could sew back into your pattern? Why not give that person a call?

If it is possible, so far as it **depends** on **you,** live **peaceably** with all.

ROMANS 12:18 NRSV

CONSIDER
THIS!

Did you know that the majority of Americans believe in miracles? In fact, a recent Newsweek poll revealed the following:

- 84 percent of Americans believe in divine miracles.

- 79 percent of Americans believe in the reality of the miracles described in the Bible.

- 48 percent of Americans have had personal experiences with miracles.

- 63 percent of Americans know others who have experienced miracles.

- 67 percent of Americans have prayed for a miracle.

God is indeed a God of miracles. What miracle are you trusting Him for in your life?

MIRACLES HAPPEN!

Can the Lord speak through a pop song? Fontella Bass thinks so. She was at the lowest ebb in her life during 1990. It had been twenty-five years since her rhythm

SORROW LOOKS BACK. WORRY LOOKS AROUND. FAITH LOOKS UP.

and blues single had hit number one on the charts. She had no career to speak of, and she was broke, tired, and cold. The only heat in her house came from a gas stove in the kitchen. She had also strayed far from the church where she started singing gospel songs as a child.

Fontella says, "I said a long prayer. I said, 'I need to see a sign to continue on.'" No sooner had she prayed than she heard her hit song, "Rescue Me," on a television commercial. To her, it was as if "the Lord had stepped right into my world!"

Fontella was unaware American Express had been using her song as part of a commercial, and officials had been unable to locate her to pay royalties. Not only did she receive back-royalties, but new opportunities began to open for her to sing.

She released a new album entitled "No Ways Tired," but the best news is that she renewed her relationship with God. "For so many years I tried doing it on my own, and it didn't work," she says. "Then I took it out of my hands and turned it over to Him, and now everything's happening."[19]

Fixing our eyes on Jesus, the author and perfecter
of faith, who for the joy set before Him
endured the cross, despising the shame, and has
sat down at the right hand of the throne of God.

HEBREWS 12:2 NASB

IT'S ALL IN YOUR PERSPECTIVE

One rainy day a woman overheard someone say, "What miserable weather!" She looked out her office window to see a big, fat robin using a nearby puddle of water for a bathtub. He was splashing and fluttering, thoroughly enjoying himself. She couldn't help but think, *Miserable for whom? It's all a matter of perspective.*

> **Some** people complain because God put thorns on roses, while others praise Him for putting roses among thorns.

That's a lesson that Lincoln Steffens learned as a young boy. He was watching an artist paint a picture of a muddy river. He told the artist he didn't like the picture because there was so much mud in it. The artist admitted there was mud in the picture, but what he saw was the beautiful colors and contrasts of the light against the dark.

Steffens later preached in a sermon, "Mud or beauty—which do we look for as we journey through life? If we look for mud and ugliness, we find them—they are there. Just as the artist found beauty in the muddy river, because that is what he was looking for, we will find, in the stream of life, those things that we desire to see. To look for the best and see the beautiful is the way to get the best out of life each day."

Even the Bible says that what you see is what you get!

Finally, brethren, whatsoever things are true, whatsoever things are honest, whatsoever things are just, whatsoever things are pure, whatsoever things are lovely, whatsoever things are of good report; if there be any virtue, and if there be any praise, think on these things.

PHILIPPIANS 4:8 KJV

#1   Have you ever taken a close look at a piece of embroidery or other needlework? On the finished side, all the threads come together perfectly, forming a beautiful picture. This side is like the wonderful plan God has for our lives. But flip the piece over, and you'll find a tangled, confused mess, illustrating how we often see our lives from our limited, human standpoint.

#2

#3   Remember, God has a beautiful plan for your life, even during those times when it seems that everything is just a big mess!

#4

#5

#6

#7

#8

#9

#10

HOW Do YOU MEASURE Up?

How would you define success?

1. The most successful people are:
   A. Those who have the biggest homes.
   B. Those who have powerful jobs.
   C. Those who live modestly and give extravagantly.

2. In their free time, truly successful people :
   A. Hang out on their yacht.
   B. Take vacations to exotic places.
   C. Invest time in their families and friends.

3. The bumper sticker that best describes successful people is:
   A. The one who dies with the most toys wins.
   B. Life is short: eat, drink, and do whatever makes you feel good.
   C. Pleasing God is job #1.

For God's definition of success, take a look through the book of Proverbs.

THE ROAD TO TRUE SUCCESS

> **I WOULD RATHER WALK WITH GOD IN THE DARK THAN GO ALONE IN THE LIGHT.**
>
> MARY GARDNER BRAINARD

On February 11, 1861, President-elect Lincoln left his home in Springfield to begin his rail journey to Washington, where he was to be inaugurated a month later. Lincoln had a premonition this would be the last time he would see Springfield. Standing on the rear platform of his railroad car, he bid the townspeople farewell. He closed his remarks with these words: "Today I leave you. I go to assume a task more difficult than that which devolved upon General Washington. The great God which guided him must help me. Without that assistance I shall surely fail; with it, I cannot fail."

The same is true for us, regardless of the tasks we face. Without God's assistance, we cannot succeed. We may get the dishes washed, the laundry folded, and the beds made. We may get our work done without accident or incident. We may find what we need at the market and manage to keep a schedule. But without God's help, our lives would be a confused mess.

Does God care about what happens in our day? Absolutely! When we become overwhelmed, making the smallest of tasks into mountains, He helps us to gather ourselves. Step-by-step, He shows us the way, and our strength is renewed to go on.

Even when **walking** through the dark **valley** of death I will **not** be **afraid,** for **you** are close beside me, **guarding,** guiding all the way.

PSALM 23:4 TLB

Whatever your hand **FINDS** to do, do it with your might.

ECCLESIASTES 9:10 NKJV

> If a task is once begun,
> never leave it till it's done.
> Be the labor great or small,
> do it well or not at all.

A JOB WELL DONE

A series of illustrations in a popular magazine once depicted the life-story of a "one-note musician." From frame to frame, the tale revealed how the woman followed her daily routine of eating and sleeping until the time came for the evening concert. She carefully inspected her music on the stand and tuned her instrument. As the concert began, the conductor skillfully cued first one group of musicians and then another until finally, the crucial moment arrived. It was time for the one note to be played!

The conductor turned to the violinist and signaled her to sound her note. She did, and then the moment was over. The orchestra played on and the "one-note" woman sat quietly through the rest of the concert—not with a sense of disappointment that she had played only one note, but with a sense of contentment and peace of mind that she had played her one note in tune, on time,

and with great gusto.

Sometimes "one-note" people are criticized for being limited or narrow in their perspective by those whose lifestyle requires the wearing of many "hats." But a job well done by others is valued by God, so it certainly deserves our recognition and respect.

Who's Who:

Johann Sebastian Bach

In 1723, Johann Sebastian Bach settled in Leipzig, Germany, where he was the director and choirmaster of Saint Thomas's church and school. Although he was a musical genius, no one recognized it. Critics said that Bach was a stuffy old man who clung stubbornly to obsolete forms of music. Consequently, he was paid only a meager salary and was unappreciated throughout the rest of his life.

Ironically, in this setting of criticism and lack of appreciation, Bach wrote his most enduring music, including The Passion of St. Matthew, which has been called the "supreme cultural achievement of all Western civilization."

For 80 years after his death, Bach and his achievements in composition went unnoticed. Like Bach, we often feel as if our work goes unnoticed and unappreciated. But if we're following God's will and doing the job that He has for us, we can be sure that He notices, and He will reward our faithfulness.

THE MARK OF A WINNER

SPORTS PSYCHOLOGISTS have identified six reoccurring traits common among gold-medal athletes. These "traits of a champion" apply to both men and women and are also dominant factors in the lives of those who succeed in non-athletic vocations.

1. Self-analysis. These successful athletes know their strengths and weaknesses and engage in critical appraisal that is honest, but never negative.

2. Self-competition. Winners know they can only control their own performances, so they compete against their own best efforts, not that of others.

3. Focus. The champion is always "in the present," concentrating on the task at hand.

4. Confidence. Successful athletes control anxiety by setting tough but reasonable goals. As goals are reached, confidence increases.

5. Toughness. This is a mental trait that involves accepting risk and trying to win, rather than trying not to lose. Winners see changes as opportunities and accept responsibility for their own destinies.

6. Having a game plan. Even elite athletes know talent is not enough. They have a game plan.[20]

Everyone can develop these traits. Everyone!

> **All our** dreams can come true—if we have the courage to pursue them.
> WALT DISNEY

Be **strong** and **courageous!** Do not be afraid or discouraged. For the LORD your God is **with** you wherever you go.

JOSHUA 1:9 NLT

new insights into ageless questions

Q

There are so many expectations placed on working women today. How will I know when I've truly become a success?

Mother Teresa of Calcutta once was asked, "How do you measure the success of your work?" She looked puzzled for a moment and then replied, "I don't remember that the Lord ever spoke of success. He spoke only of faithfulness in love. This is the only success that really matters." As Mother Teresa suggests, whatever career we've chosen in life—teacher, homemaker, doctor, salesclerk—it's really secondary in importance to the number one job He's given us, which is to be faithful in love. Consider the apostle Paul, for example. He was a tentmaker by trade, but we don't know him today because of his tent-making career. We know him because he dedicated his life in faithfulness and love to others. If you excel at your primary job—serving others, faithfully and lovingly—then you will be a true winner in God's eyes. And that's the only success that really matters.

OUR TRUE VALUE

A saleswoman passed a particular corner each day on her way to work. For more than a week she observed a young girl trying to sell a floppy-eared puppy. The saleswoman finally said to the girl, "Honey, if you really want to sell this dog, then I suggest you clean him up, brush his coat, raise your price, and make people think they're getting something big." At noon, the saleswoman noticed the girl had taken her advice. The puppy was groomed and sitting under a big sign: "TREEMENNDOUS Puppy for Sale—$5,000."

The saleswoman smiled and gulped, determined to tell the girl later that she may have overpriced the puppy. To her surprise, on the way home she saw the puppy was gone! Flabbergasted, the woman sought out the girl to ask if she had really sold the dog for $5,000.

The girl replied, "I sure did, and I want to thank you for all your help." The saleswoman stuttered, "How in the world did you do it?" The girl said, "It was easy. I just took two $2,500 cats in exchange!"

Two thousand years ago there was another great exchange. On a cross outside Jerusalem, Jesus Christ gave His life in exchange for ours. What value did He see in us? We were His prized creation, stolen for a season by our own will, but now repurchased as His beloved possession.

IF YOU DON'T STAND FOR SOMETHING YOU'LL FALL FOR ANYTHING!

YOU WERE BOUGHT WITH A PRICE;
THEREFORE GLORIFY GOD IN YOUR BODY AND
IN YOUR SPIRIT, WHICH ARE GOD'S.

1 CORINTHIANS 6:20 NKJV

WISE WORDS

Be absolutely certain that our Lord loves
you, devotedly and individually, loves
you just as you are… Accustom yourself
to the wonderful thought that God loves
you with a tenderness, a generosity, and
an intimacy that surpasses all your
dreams. Give yourself up with joy to a
loving confidence in God and have
courage to believe firmly that God's action toward you is a masterpiece of par-
tiality and love. Rest tranquilly in this
abiding conviction.

HENRI DE TOURVILLE

Fun Trivia

The body's immune system relies on the partnership between what medical scientists have labeled T cells and B cells. Like microscopic "watchmen," T cells, produced in the thymus gland, monitor the blood and trigger an alarm when they detect something suspicious. Immediately, B cells, produced in the bone marrow, go into action, seeking out the invader and attacking it. Because of this well-oiled partnership between the T and B cells, our bodies are able to combat all kinds of germs—from those that cause the common cold to those that cause wounds to get infected.

Likewise, God has given our minds a protection against things that would harm us. Our conscience is an inner monitor, detecting and warning us against destructive and ungodly thoughts and desires. When we heed its warnings, then exercise our will to avoid the danger, we are building up our "immunity" to thoughts and actions that are unpleasing to God.

LET YOUR CONSCIENCE GUIDE YOU

There is **one** thing alone
that **stands** the **brunt** of life
throughout its length:
a quiet conscience. EURIPEDES

President Woodrow Wilson was approached one day by one of his secretaries, who suggested he take off from his work to enjoy a particular diversion he enjoyed. President Wilson replied, "My boss won't let me do it."

"Your boss?" the secretary asked, wondering who could be the boss of the chief executive of the United States.

"Yes," said Wilson. "I have a conscience that is my boss. It drives me to the task, and it will not let me accept this tempting invitation."

Our conscience is one of the most prized items we posses. It is through our conscience we receive inner promptings from God which, when in agreement with our actions, will point us toward a safe and eternal way.

It has been said, "A conscience is like a thermostat on an air conditioning unit—it kicks in when things are on the verge of getting too hot."

It is possible to ignore our conscience and "follow the crowd," but this is a sad waste of our lives. The conscience is the window to the soul through which we hear the voice of God, Who always leads us to success and inner peace.

Listen carefully, He may have something good to say!

If our **hearts** do not **condemn** us,
we have **confidence** before God

1 JOHN 3:21 NIV

TRUSTING IN GOD'S GOODNESS

> MOST **PEOPLE** WISH TO **SERVE** GOD— BUT ONLY IN AN **ADVISORY** CAPACITY.

FOR WEEKS, eight-year-old Susie had been looking forward to a particular Saturday fishing trip with her dad. But when the day finally arrived, it was raining heavily.

Susie wandered around the house all morning, grumbling as she peered out the windows, "Seems like the Lord would know it would have been better to have the rain yesterday than today." Her father tried to explain how important the rain was to the farmers and gardeners. But Susie only replied, "It just isn't fair."

Around three o'clock, the rain stopped. There was still time for fishing, so father and daughter quickly loaded their gear and headed for the lake.

Because of the rainstorm, the fish were really biting. Within a couple of hours, they returned with a full stringer of fish.

At the family's fish dinner that night, Susie was asked to say grace. She concluded her prayer by saying, "And, Lord, if I sounded grumpy earlier today, it was because I couldn't see far enough ahead."[21]

When we seek God's advice in our lives, it is important to realize He alone can see what's coming!

You will keep in perfect **peace** him whose **mind** is **steadfast**, because he **trusts** in you.

ISAIAH 26:3 NIV

TOP 10 LIST

Benefits of Trusting God

The next time you are having trouble trusting God, read Psalm 37.
It is loaded with the benefits of putting your complete trust in Him, including:

1. RECEIVING THE DESIRES OF YOUR HEART (VERSE 4)

2. **BEING VINDICATED (VERSES 5-6)**

3. ENJOYING GREAT PEACE (VERSE 11)

4. **BEING UPHELD BY GOD (VERSE 17)**

5. ENJOYING PLENTY IN DAYS OF WANT (VERSE 19)

6. **ALWAYS LIVING SECURELY (VERSE 24)**

7. NEVER BEING FORSAKEN BY GOD (VERSE 28)

8. **SEEING THE WICKED CUT OFF (VERSE 34)**

9. HAVING A FUTURE (VERSE 37)

10. **BEING HELPED AND DELIVERED BY THE LORD (VERSE 40)**

What other benefits of trusting God do you find in this powerful psalm?

WAIT FOR HIS GIFT

Author Elisabeth Elliot writes in *A Lamp for My Feet* about a game she played as a young girl. She writes, "My mother or father would say, 'Shut your eyes and hold out your hand.' That was the promise of some lovely surprise. I trusted them, so I shut my eyes instantly and held out my hand. Whatever they were going to give me I was ready to take." She continues, "So should it be in our trust of our heavenly Father. Faith is the willingness to receive whatever He wants to give, or the willingness not to have what He does not want to give."[22]

> **God always** gives His best to those who leave the choice with Him. JIM ELLIOT

If your prayers aren't answered in the way you expect them to be, there may be a good reason! Several months before Christmas, Jared begged his mother to buy him a new bicycle just like his friend's—and he had to have it now. His mother was a single mom, however, and there was no extra money for a new bicycle until Christmas.

Jared's friend generously lent him his bicycle to ride, and the longer Jared rode it, the more he realized it really wasn't the right bicycle for him. For one thing, it didn't have the racing brakes he wanted.

How often do we think God has forgotten us, when He's merely giving us time to understand what we really want and bringing us His best?

Blessed be the Lord, who **daily** bears us up;

God is our **salvation**.

PSALM 86:19 NRSV

☑ JUST DO IT

#1   An answer to prayer is one of the greatest gifts God gives us. To keep track of all the creative ways God has answered your prayer requests, keep a prayer journal. Any journal or notebook will do. Simply record a prayer request on each page, along with the date. (Of course, some requests may be repeated many times.) When you sense God has answered your prayer, even if His answer is "no" or "not yet," make a note of the answer and the date. Over a period of time you will collect many requests and answers. When you look back over your notes you'll discover all the ways God responds, and you'll be encouraged to realize that if there's a prayer He doesn't seem to be answering yet, there's probably a very good reason for the delay.

#2

#3

#4

#5

#6

#7

#8

#9

#10

"Faith is not belief without PROOF, but trust without reservation."

ELTON TRUEBLOOD

> I have no regrets. I couldn't be more sure of
> my ground—the One I've trusted in can take care of
> what he's trusted me to do right to the end.
>
> 2 TIMOTHY 1:12 MSG

TRUST AND OBEY

During the terrible days of the Blitz in World War II, a father—holding his young daughter by the hand—ran from a building that had been struck by a bomb. In the front yard was a large hole left by a shell explosion several days before. Seeking shelter as quickly as possible, the father jumped into the hole and then held up his arms for his young daughter to follow.

Terrified at the explosions around her and unable to see her father in the darkness of the hole, she cried, "I can't see you, Papa!"

The father looked up against the sky that was lit with white tracer lights and tinted red by burning buildings and called to his daughter, who was standing in silhouette at the hole's edge, "But I can see you, my darling. Jump!"

The little girl jumped . . . not because she could see her father, but because she trusted him to tell her the truth and to do what was best for her.

We may not be able to discern clearly where it is our Heavenly Father is leading us, but we can trust it is to a good place. We may not know what God has "up His sleeve," but we can trust His arms to be everlasting.

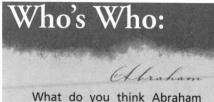

Who's Who:

Abraham

What do you think Abraham was thinking when God told him to send the handmaiden Hagar and Ishmael, his son by her, away? That he was able to obey God at that moment and send them away with just a skin of water and some bread speaks to the fact that Abraham and God were in constant contact. Abraham trusted God because he knew God well, and because he trusted in God's promises. This relationship was put to the test again when God asked Abraham to sacrifice his son Isaac. As painful as it was, Abraham was prepared to obey right up until God stepped in. We will trust Him when we know Him, and we will obey once we trust.

HOW Do YOU MEASURE Up?

There are lots of warning systems in life. How well do you pay attention to them? Take this quiz to find out.

1. When I pull last season's clothes out of storage and most don't fit, I:
   A. Go on a shopping spree and indulge in a whole new wardrobe.
   B. Become depressed about my weight gain, and go out for ice cream to feel better.
   C. Make a commitment to diet and exercise and stick with it.

2. When the fire alarm in the hallway begins to chirp, indicating the need for a fresh battery, I:
   A. Ignore it and hope someone else will take care of it.
   B. Pull it off the wall and stash it in the closet.
   C. Change the battery immediately.

3. When the Holy Spirit convicts me about something I've done wrong, I:
   A. Make excuses for my behavior.
   B. Ignore Him—after all, nobody's perfect!
   C. Confess, repent, and, if necessary, make reparations to anyone I've hurt.

PAY ATTENTION TO THE WARNINGS

CONSCIENCE IS GOD'S BUILT-IN WARNING SYSTEM. BE VERY HAPPY WHEN IT HURTS YOU. BE VERY WORRIED WHEN IT DOESN'T.

Kelley was surprised to find a hair dryer tucked into a corner of an old suitcase. For years she had used the case to store bits of fabric from her sewing projects. Now, while piecing together a quilt, she had unearthed it. *Where did this come from?* she asked herself.

After several days of trying to remember, she recalled having used it while visiting friends nearly a decade before. She had made several visits to the family and apparently had placed the borrowed hair dryer into her case inadvertently. To complicate matters, the family had asked about its whereabouts, and she had replied she didn't have a clue!

Embarrassed, she thought, *How can I tell my friends after all these years that I have this?* However, her conscience wouldn't let the matter rest. She finally sent the hair dryer back to the family with an apology and an explanation. With many laughs, all was quickly forgiven.

A healthy conscience is one of our greatest gifts from God. It serves to keep our lives on track and thus maintains peace in our hearts.

The **integrity** of the upright **guides** them.

PROVERBS 11:3 NIV

GOD'S UNEXPECTED PROVISION

Victor Frankl was stripped of everything he owned when he was arrested by the Nazis in World War II. He arrived at Auschwitz with only his manuscript—a book he had been researching and writing for years—sewn into the lining of his coat. Upon arrival, even that was taken from him. He later wrote, "I had to undergo and overcome the loss of my spiritual child. . . . It seemed as if nothing and no one would survive me. I found myself confronted with the question of whether under such circumstances my life was ultimately void of any meaning."

Days later, the Nazis forced the prisoners to give up their clothes. In return Frankl was given rags of an inmate who had been sent to the gas chamber. In the pocket of the garment he found a torn piece of paper—a page from a Hebrew prayer book. On it was the foremost Jewish prayer, "Shema Yisrael" which begins, "Hear, O Israel! The Lord our God is one God."

Frankl says, "How should I have interpreted such a 'coincidence' other than as a challenge to live my thoughts instead of merely putting them on paper?" He later wrote in his classic masterpiece, *Man's Search for Meaning,* "He who has a why to live for can bear almost any how."[23]

> A COINCIDENCE IS A SMALL MIRACLE WHERE GOD PREFERS TO REMAIN ANONYMOUS.

WHO CAN PUT INTO WORDS AND TELL THE MIGHTY DEEDS OF THE LORD? OR CAN SHOW FORTH ALL THE PRAISE [THAT IS DUE HIM]?

PSALM 106:2 AMP

WISE WORDS

God is never in a panic,
nothing can be done that
he is not absolute Master
of, and no one in earth or
heaven can shut a door he
has opened, nor open a
door he has shut. God al-
ters the inevitable when
we get in touch with him.

OSWALD CHAMBERS

booklist

THE FOUNTAIN OF JOY

IN A MATTER OF SECONDS, Vickie's life was shattered. A trapeze artist, she lost control of the flybar one day and careened headfirst into the net. She broke her neck between the fifth and sixth cervical vertebrae and became paralyzed, a quadriplegic.

Three years after the accident, she had fallen into deep despair and self-pity and was determined to take her life. Her attempt failed, and she ended up in a psychiatric hospital. On the fourth anniversary of her fall, she and her husband separated. Bitterness set in.

One day a Christian home health aide was assigned to her. Mae Lynne introduced Vickie to Jesus Christ and the Bible.

Vickie began to learn to "stand firm" in her faith and to "walk" in obedience to God.

A minister faithfully taught her for two years. Then Vickie began a ministry of encouragement by writing a dozen letters each week to prison inmates and others with disabilities. She now says, "Quadriplegics aren't supposed to have this much joy, are they?"[24]

Vickie still uses a wheelchair, becomes dizzy at times, has occasional respiratory problems, and needs an attendant's care. However, she has deep inner strength because of her relationship with Jesus. Now others describe her as "a fountain of smiles."

> **Content-ment** isn't getting what we want but being satisfied with what we have.

Paul said, "I've learned by now to be quite content whatever my circumstances."

PHILIPPIANS 4:11 MSG

CONSIDER
THIS!

When we show lovingkindness to children, they are more likely to pass it on. A story is told about a mother who watched from her kitchen window as her young son walked across the yard to visit with the elderly gentleman next door who had recently lost his wife. After a while, she saw her little boy climb up into the old man's lap and put his head against the man's chest. He seemed to sit there for a long while before finally crawling down and coming home for supper.

"That was nice of you to visit our neighbor, honey," the mother said to the little boy at the supper table. "I know he's very sad right now. What did you say to him?"

"I didn't say anything to him," the little boy replied. "I just helped him cry."

CHILDREN LEARN WHAT THEY LIVE

Kindness provides a house, but love makes a home.

Kindness packs an adequate sack lunch, but love puts a note of encouragement inside.

Kindness provides a television set or computer as a learning aid, but love controls the remote control and cares enough to insist a child "sign off."

Kindness sends a child to bed on time, but love tucks the covers around a child's neck and provides a goodnight hug and kiss.

Kindness cooks a meal, but love selects the "your favorite foods" menu and lights the candles.

Kindness writes a thank-you

THE TEACHER ASKED THE PUPILS TO TELL THE MEANING OF LOVINGKINDNESS. A LITTLE BOY JUMPED UP AND SAID, "WELL, IF I WAS HUNGRY AND SOMEONE GAVE ME A PIECE OF BREAD THAT WOULD BE KINDNESS. BUT IF THEY PUT A LITTLE JELLY ON IT, THAT WOULD BE LOVINGKINDNESS."

note, but love thinks to include a joke or photograph or bookmark inside the envelope.

Kindness keeps a clean and tidy house, but love adds a bouquet of fresh flowers.

Kindness pours a glass of milk, but love occasionally adds a little chocolate sauce.

Kindness is doing what is decent, basic, courteous, and necessary for an even, smooth, and gentle flow of life.

Love is taking the extra step to make life truly exciting, creative, and meaningful. Love is what makes things special.

Bless the Lord, O my soul; . . . who redeems your life from destruction, who crowns you with lovingkindness and tender mercies.

PSALM 103:1,4 NKJV

ENDURING THE TOUGH TIMES

Many people see abundant spring rains as a great blessing to farmers, especially if the rains come after the plants have sprouted and are several inches tall. What they don't realize is even a short drought can have a devastating effect on a crop of seedlings that have received too much rain.

> **You should** never let adversity get you down— except on your knees.

Why? Because during frequent rains, the young plants are not required to push their roots deeper into the soil in search of water. If a drought occurs later, plants with shallow root systems will quickly die.

We often receive abundance into our lives—rich fellowship, great teaching, thorough "soakings" of spiritual blessings. Yet, when stress or tragedy enters our lives, we may find ourselves thinking God has abandoned us or is unfaithful. The fact is, we have allowed the easiness of our lives to keep us from pushing our spiritual roots deeper. We have allowed others to spoon-feed us, rather than developing our own deep, personal relationship with God through prayer and study of His Word.

Only the deeply rooted are able to endure hard times without wilting. The best advice is to enjoy the "rain" while seeking to grow even closer to Him.

I am persuaded, that neither death, nor life, nor angels, nor principalities, nor powers, nor things present, nor things to come . . . will be able to separate us from the love of God, which is in Christ Jesus our Lord.

ROMANS 8:38,39 NASB

☑ JUST DO IT

#1   You probably know a woman who has faced adversity in life and come out stronger and more committed to God. She may be an ordinary woman who has used her struggles to make herself better rather than bitter. Invite her to lunch or for coffee. Ask her advice about how to triumph over adversity. What did she do? How did she pray? Does she have any favorite verses to share? Perhaps she might be willing to mentor you through any problems you're currently facing.

#2

#3

#4

#5

#6

#7

#8

#9

#10

TURNING FROM TEMPTATION

SALLY WAS TRYING desperately to save all the pennies she could for the doll carriage she wanted to buy. She was turning in aluminum cans, offering to do extra chores . . . anything to make a few more cents a week.

One night as she was saying her bedtime prayers, her mother overheard Sally say in great earnest, "O Lord, please help me to save my money for the doll carriage in Mr. Brown's store window. It's so beautiful, and I want it so much. It's just right for my doll. And I'd be sure to let my friends play with it too."

Pleased by her daughter's prayer, Sally's mother was star-tled to hear the final line of the prayer. "And please God, don't let the ice cream man come down our street this week!"

Just as we are each unique in our talents, abilities, background, and experiences, we are also unique in what tempts us. What is tempting to one person may not be at all tempting to another.

Although the enemy of our souls knows our weak points, we know our Strength—Jesus. As we stick close to Him, when temptation comes, we can draw on His strength to turn from it.

Always say yes to Jesus, and saying no to temptation will become easy!

> **When** you flee temptations don't leave a forwarding address.

Now flee from youthful lusts and pursue righteousness, faith, love and peace, with those who call on the Lord from a pure heart.

2 TIMOTHY 2:22 NASB

I understand how to avoid temptation when it comes to the things that are evil in God's sight or things that are bad for me. Where I struggle is that I'm often tempted to say yes to too many positive, good things, and I end up over-scheduled and stressed. Why am I tempted to say yes when I know I should say no?

Many people are tempted by opportunities to feel needed, and so they say yes whenever they are asked to serve on a committee, bake a meal, or pick up a friend at the airport— even when it puts their sanity at risk! Seeing this tendency as another form of temptation is the first step. Just as with other temptations, ask God to be a buffer between you and the thing that is tempting you. Call on His strength to say no, and He will give you the words to do it tactfully but forcefully. Once you embrace His acceptance, which has always been there for you, your need to be needed by others in a compulsive, destructive way will dissipate.

"A day hemmed in **PRAYER** is less likely to **unravel**."

ANONYMOUS

> **Pray about everything; tell God your needs and don't forget to thank him for his answers. If you do this, you will experience God's peace. . . . His peace will keep your thoughts and your hearts quiet and at rest.**
>
> PHILIPPIANS 4:6,7 TLB

PRAY WITHOUT CEASING

It was 2 A.M. when a weary traveler landed in Tahiti. Her flight from Hawaii had been a turbulent one, causing a delay in her arrival on the island. The stormy skies had also forced her connecting flight to a nearby island to be cancelled, forcing her to make plans to spend at least a day near the airport. An hour later, she found herself standing with her luggage in a small but clean motel room, totally exhausted after more than twenty-four hours of travel. Her mind, however, refused to stop racing with concern about whom to call and what to do.

The woman was on a short-term missionary trip to help set up a clinic on a remote South Seas island. Now she was beginning to wonder if she had heard God correctly! At that hour, and as weary as she was, she felt alone at the edge of the world. Glancing down at her watch, she saw it read 11 A.M.—the time her Bible study group had said they would be in prayer for her. *They're praying right now!* she thought, and suddenly, she felt deep peace and comfort. Within minutes, she was sound asleep.

When you are feeling as if you are about to unravel inside, turn to prayer. The travel route of prayer is never misdirected or put off schedule—nor is it dangerous! On the contrary, prayer gives peace and helps us avoid danger.

Who's Who:

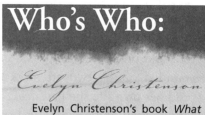
Evelyn Christenson

Evelyn Christenson's book *What Happens When Women Pray* has sold over two million copies worldwide. Evelyn has been leading prayer seminars since 1968 and has spoken to hundreds of thousands of people from local congregations to prayer conferences to the World Congress on Evangelism.

But Evelyn knows it is only by God's strength that she is able to spread His message about prayer—and only because she prays herself. Once before a major speaking event Evelyn was suffering from a terribly sore throat and was in danger of losing her voice completely. She remembers kneeling down in her hotel room and praying for the Lord to help her recover to the point that she could still give her talk, and she credits Him completely with the fact that she spoke that night.

CHERISH THE GIFT OF LIFE

> THE SECRET OF **CONTENTMENT** IS THE REALIZATION THAT **LIFE** IS A **GIFT**, NOT A RIGHT.

FORMER nationally syndicated columnist and current author, Anna Quindlen, seems to have enjoyed success at everything she has attempted. But in taking a fellow commentator to task after he made light of teenage problems, Anna was reminded of the two attempts to end her own life she had made at age sixteen. She writes, "I was really driven through my high school years. I always had to be perfect in every way, ranging from how I looked to how my grades were. It was too much pressure."

In the early 1970s, Anna's mother died from ovarian cancer.

This tragedy cured Anna from any desire to commit suicide. Her attitude toward life changed. "I could never look at life as anything but a great gift. I realized I didn't have any business taking it for granted."[25]

It is only when we recognize life as "temporary" that we truly come to grips with what is important. When we face our own immortality, our priorities quickly come into focus.

Consider your life as God's gift to you. Every moment is precious, so cherish each one. In doing so, you'll find purpose and meaning for each day.

Godliness with contentment is great gain. For we brought nothing into this world, and it is certain we can carry nothing out.

1 TIMOTHY 6:6-7 NKJV

TOP **10** TIPS

for Keeping Your Life Meaningful

1. CARE MORE ABOUT OTHERS THAN ABOUT THINGS.

2. **GIVE YOURSELF TO SERVE RATHER THAN TO BE SERVED.**

3. SPEND TIME READING GOD'S WORD RATHER THAN WATCHING TV.

4. SPEND AS MUCH TIME WITH YOUR FAMILY AS YOU DO AT YOUR JOB.

5. DEPEND ON GOD RATHER THAN YOURSELF.

6. **STORE UP TREASURE IN HEAVEN RATHER THAN ON EARTH.**

7. BE CONTENT WITH WHAT YOU HAVE.

8. DO AT LEAST ONE KIND DEED EVERY DAY.

9. DON'T ALLOW YOURSELF TO BE UPSET BY LITTLE THINGS.

10. **LIVE IN A CONSTANT STATE OF PRAYER.**

CITIZENS OF HEAVEN

Before the colonialists imposed national boundaries, the kings of Laos and Vietnam had already reached an agreement about who was Laotian and who was Vietnamese. Those who ate short-grain rice, built their houses on stilts, and decorated their homes with Indian-style serpents were considered Laotians. Those who ate long-grain rice, built their houses on the ground, and decorated their homes with Chinese-style dragons were Vietnamese. The kings taxed the people accordingly, and had little use for boundaries apart from this designation.

The kings knew it was not the exact location of a person's home that determined their culture of loyalty. Instead, each person belonged to the kingdom whose values they shared.

So it is with a Christian. Regardless of our culture or nationality, we belong to God's kingdom. We live according to the values, standards, and commandments He has established. When we pray, "Thy kingdom come, Thy will be done," we are asking that the heavenly law of love become established in our lives here on earth. We are His people, regardless of our address.

IT'S GOOD TO BE A CHRISTIAN AND KNOW IT, BUT IT'S BETTER TO BE A CHRISTIAN AND SHOW IT!

JESUS SAID, "BY THIS EVERYONE WILL KNOW THAT YOU ARE MY DISCIPLES, IF YOU HAVE LOVE FOR ONE ANOTHER."

JOHN 13:35 NRSV

WISE WORDS

In ancient times, an anonymous person wrote a letter in which he described a strange new kind of people who called themselves Christians. In the letter, today known as the "Letter to Diognetus," he wrote:

"Christians are not differentiated from other people by country, language, or customs; you see, they do not live in cities of their own, or speak some strange dialect. They live in both Greek and foreign cities, wherever chance has put them. They follow local customs in clothing, food, and the other aspects of life. But at the same time, they demonstrate to us the unusual form of their own citizenship.

"They marry and have children just like everyone else, but they do not kill unwanted babies. They offer a shared table, but not a shared bed. They are passing their days on earth, but are citizens of heaven. They obey the appointed laws and go beyond the laws in their own lives.

"They love everyone, but are persecuted by all. They are put to death and gain life. They are poor and yet make many rich. They are dishonored and yet gain glory through dishonor. Their names are blackened, and yet they are cleared. They are mocked and bless in return. They are treated outrageously and behave respectfully to others. When they do good, they are punished as evildoers; when punished, they rejoice as if being given new life."

Fun Trivia

All of us have seen geese flying in "V" formation, but do you know why they do this? As each goose flaps its wings, it creates an uplift for the one following it. Flying in this formation allows the geese to travel much farther than they could on their own. When the lead goose gets tired, it rotates to another position in the formation, and another goose takes over. The honking that you hear is actually the geese encouraging those in the lead to keep up their speed.

Geese flying in formation are a beautiful picture of how God wants us to support each other. We are called not only to encourage those in the lead, but also to do our part to serve one another and help lighten the load of those who are tired.

DO UNTO OTHERS

The **greatest** achievements are
those that **benefit** others.

DENNIS WAITLEY

A recent plot of the soap opera *All My Children* called for high-society philanthropist Brooke English to move into a homeless shelter to better understand their plight. Julia Barr, who plays Brooke, felt prompted by the part to take some real-life action of her own. She became a participant in First Step, a New York City job-readiness program for homeless and formerly homeless women. The eight-week session included one-on-one mentoring, résumé advice, access to job internships, interview clothing, and pep talks from people such as herself.

Says Julia, "I know how it feels to lack motivation and self-esteem. I tend to procrastinate; I'm rarely on time; I'm rather bossy; I'm very stubborn—we all have things that hold us back, and so I share mine."[26]

Julia is not only giving her time but also her money. When her maternal grandmother, Myrtle, died at the age of 104, she left Julia a nice amount of money. It was all donated to First Step.

Julia Barr has one Emmy award and six nominations, but those in First Step will remember her for the care she gave to them.

"To be the greatest,
be a servant."

MATTHEW 23:11 TLB

HOW Do YOU MEASURE Up?

The way we respond to upsetting events can reveal a great deal about whether we have the peace of the Lord. Consider the following questions:

When someone is an hour late getting home, I:
   A. Think about how upset I am about being inconvenienced.
   B. Begin listening for sirens because I'm sure they were involved in a wreck.
   C. Assume the person is unavoidably delayed, but all right.

When the boss says he or she needs to see me first thing in the morning, I:
   A. Stay awake all night worried that I might be getting fired.
   B. Think about whom I can blame for whatever has gone wrong.
   C. Sleep soundly knowing that whatever happens, the Lord is in control.

When I have a splitting headache for two days straight, I:
   A. Assume I have a brain tumor and begin planning my funeral.
   B. Try to ignore it and hope it goes away.
   C. Take an appropriate dose of pain reliever and rest.

If there were lots of A and B answers to these questions, you may have to ask God for help in setting your worry aside and trusting Him to see you through the circumstances in your life.

FIND PEACE IN THE LORD

SOMETIMES THE LORD CALMS THE STORM; SOMETIMES HE LETS THE STORM RAGE AND CALMS HIS CHILD.

In *Especially for a Woman,* Beverly LaHaye writes about how upset she was when her husband, Tim, told her he wanted to take flying lessons. Her quick response was, "I think you're foolish! Why would you want to get into a plane with only one engine?"

Tim asked her to pray about the matter, but she writes, "I started right off giving God my opinions and drawing my own conclusions. My fear . . . was controlling me." Tim suggested, "Be open with the Lord. . . . Let Him know you're afraid of flying, but that you're willing to be changed if that's what He would have."

Beverly did just that. Tim took flying lessons, and repeatedly she committed her fears—and their lives—to the Lord.

Years later she was a passenger in a commuter plane that was caught in a storm. As the plane bounced in the sky, the LaHaye's attorney—normally a very calm man—felt sure they were going to crash. Then he looked over and saw that Beverly was asleep! He asked her later, "How could you sleep so peacefully?"

Beverly responded, "It has to be God. Only He could have brought me from that crippling fearfulness . . . to a place where I could fly through such a storm and be at peace."[27]

The **peace** of God, which transcends all understanding, will guard your hearts and your minds in Christ Jesus.

PHILIPPIANS 4:7 NIV

THE SWEET SOUND
OF "SORRY"

In 1755 a twenty-three-year-old colonel was in the midst of running for a seat in the Virginia assembly when he made an insulting remark as part of a campaign speech. The remark was addressed to a hot-tempered man named Payne, who responded by knocking the colonel down with a hickory stick. Soldiers rushed to the colonel's assistance, and it appeared that a full-blown fight would ensue. But the would-be politician got up, dusted himself off, called off the soldiers, and left the scene.

> **The best** way to get the last word is to apologize.

The next morning the colonel wrote Payne, requesting his presence at a local tavern. Payne obliged, but wondered what motives and demands the colonel might make—perhaps an apology or even a duel. To Payne's surprise, the colonel met him with an apology, asking forgiveness for his derogatory remarks and offering a handshake.

The move may have been viewed by others as politically expedient, but Colonel George Washington considered it personally imperative if he was to enjoy internal peace as he continued with his campaign.

The moment we feel like demanding forgiveness from others may be the moment when we are to forgive.

If you are snared in the utterance of your lips, caught in the words of your mouth; then do this, my son, and save yourself, for you have come into your neighbor's power: go, hasten, and importune yourself with your neighbor.

PROVERBS 6:2-3 RSV

#1 Often the need for an apology is the result of hurtful words that we've carelessly let fall from our lips. The next

#2 time you're near a pond or puddle, drop a stone into the water. Observe the ripples that spread out, farther and farther, and be reminded of the "ripple effect" of careless, hurt-ful words. Is there anyone you've hurt recently with your

#3 words? Unlike the ripples from a stone dropped into water, you can stop the ripples of hurt feelings by offering a sincere apology. If you find it hard to apologize, begin by apologiz-ing to God. After all, when you hurt one of His children, you

#4 hurt Him as well. Then ask Him for courage and the right words to say to the individual you have harmed.

#5

#6

#7

#8

CHOOSE YOUR WORDS CAREFULLY

WHILE IN MEDICAL TRAINing, surgeons are encouraged to weigh the importance of each word spoken during an operation. As the anesthetic is given, fear may strike a patient if she hears someone say, "I'm going to shoot her now." Even a phrase such as "hook up the monitor" may be interpreted by a drugged patient as sounding like "shake up the monster." Can you imagine the impact on a half-dazed patient if she hears a doctor say, "This isn't my day!"

The same directions given by two different physicians could encourage or discourage a patient, simply by their tone of voice. One doctor's voice might suggest a prescription will work, while another's voice might convey reservations. Either would drastically affect the morale of a patient.

Theodore Roosevelt popularized an expression about the need for clear, precise communication. He called words with several possible meanings "weasel words"— by using them a speaker might weasel out of any commitment, claiming a different interpretation of the word.

The Bible also tells us again and again to remember the importance of our words. We are always to speak words of encouragement, hope, and faith to those around us.

ighten up

Verbal bloopers are always embarrassing, but take comfort, even the most educated and eloquent of us sometimes say the wrong thing. The Massachusetts Bar Association Lawyers Journal recently printed the following questions actually asked by lawyers of witnesses during a trial:

- Now, doctor, isn't it true that when a person dies in his sleep, he doesn't know about it until the next morning?
- The youngest son, the 20-year-old, how old is he?
- Were you present when your picture was taken?
- Were you alone or by yourself?
- Was it you or your younger brother who was killed in the army?
- How far apart were the vehicles at the time of the collision?
- You were there until the time you left, is that true?

Jesus said, "Let your statement be,

"No" is one of the few words that can never be misunderstood. "

'Yes, yes' or 'No, no.'" MATTHEW 5:37 NASB

I call on the
LORD in my distress,
and he answers me.

PSALM 120:1 NIV

Look around you and be distressed, look within you and be depressed, look to Jesus and be at rest.

HELP IS A PRAYER AWAY

The 911 emergency system has amazing capabilities. In most places in the United States, a person need only dial those three numbers to be instantly connected to a dispatcher. On a computer screen the dispatcher instantly sees the caller's telephone number, address, and the name under which the number is listed. Also listening in on the call are police, fire, and paramedic assistants. A caller need not say anything once the call is made. Even rasping coughs and hysterical cries have brought a quick response. The dispatcher knows where the call is coming from, and help is sent.

At times, some situations in our lives are so desperate and our pain so deep we can only muster a 911 prayer to God. These are called "SOS prayers," and they often use the same words: "God, I need help!" God hears each one. He knows our names and every detail of the situations. Like a heavenly dispatcher, He will send precisely who is needed to assist us.

Also like a 911 dispatcher, our Heavenly Dispatcher may have some advice to sustain us through a crisis. Keep a listening ear and remember, help is on the way!

Who's Who:

Thomas Merton

Thomas Merton, an American Trappist monk and poet, has offered inspiration and strength to millions through his writings and the witness of his life. His autobiography, *The Seven Storey Mountain*, appears on lists of the 100 most important books of the century. Reflect on this famous prayer by Merton:

My Lord God,
I have no idea where I am going. I do not see the road ahead of me. I cannot know for certain where it will end. Nor do I really know myself, and the fact that I think that I am following Your will does not mean that I am actually doing so.

But I believe that the desire to please You does in fact please You. And I hope I have that desire in all that I am doing. I hope that I will never do anything apart from that desire. And I know that if I do this You will lead me by the right road though I may know nothing about it.

Therefore, will I trust You always though I may seem to be lost and in the shadow of death. I will not fear, You are ever with me, and You will never leave me to face my perils alone.

SEEK THE KINGDOM FIRST

A pastor's wife was amazed when she heard a person say, "One hour is only 4 percent of a day." She had not thought about time in this way. Sensing the need for more prayer time in her life, she thought surely she could give God at least 4 percent of her time. She determined to try it.

BE MORE CONCERNED WITH WHAT GOD THINKS ABOUT YOU THAN WHAT PEOPLE THINK ABOUT YOU.

Rather than try to fit prayer into her schedule, she decided to fix a prayer time, and then fit the rest of the day around it. At the time, her children were old enough to travel to school alone. By 8:30 each morning, a hush fell over her home. She knew her best hour for prayer would be between 8:30 and 9:30 A.M. To guarantee she was uninterrupted, she made it known in the parish that, except for emergencies, she would be grateful if people didn't call her until 9:30 in the morning.

To her surprise, no one in the church was offended. Instead they responded very positively. Several other women began to follow her example by setting aside the same hour to pray every day!

When we seek God's plan first, all our plans with other people will have a way of falling into place.

"SEEK FIRST THE KINGDOM OF GOD AND HIS RIGHTEOUSNESS, AND ALL THESE THINGS SHALL BE ADDED TO YOU."

MATTHEW 6:33 NKJV

WISE WORDS

Jesus did not say, "Come to Me and get it over with." He said, "If any man would come after Me, let him take up his cross daily and follow Me." Daily is the key word. Our commitment to Christ, however genuine and whole-hearted it may be today, must be renewed tomorrow . . . and the day after that . . . and the day after that.

LOUIS CASSELS

USING YOUR GIFTS

ONE OF THE ITEMS IN *Ripley's Believe It or Not* is a picture of a plain bar of iron. It is valued at $5. The same bar of iron has a far different value, however, if it is fashioned into different items.

• As a pair of horseshoes, it would be worth $50.

• As sewing needles, it would be worth $5,000.

• As balance springs for fine Swiss watches, it would be worth $500,000.

The raw material is not what is important. What's important is how raw material is developed. Each of us has been given talents and abilities—some have received more, others less, but all have received something as a unique gift from God. As Christians, we also enjoy spiritual gifts which flow from the Holy Spirit of God.

The value of these raw materials, however, is a moot point unless we develop and use our talents, abilities, and spiritual gifts as a force for divine good in this world.

If you don't know what your abilities and gifts are, ask God to reveal them to you. Then ask Him to show you what He wants you to do with them. Your happiness and success in life will be found in fulfilling His plan for your life.

> **God never** asks about our ability or our inability —just our availability.

I heard the voice of the Lord, saying, Whom shall I send, and who will go for us? Then said I, Here am I; send me.

ISAIAH 6:8 KJV

I want to use my spiritual gifts, but I don't know if I have any. If I do, I don't know what they are. How can I find out?

First of all, be assured that if you have accepted Jesus Christ as your Lord and Savior, you received at least one spiritual gift at that time. (For clarification, read 1 Corinthians 12:4-7, Romans 12:6-8, Ephesians 4:11-13, and 1 Peter 4:10-11.)

Once you have established in your heart that God has given you a gift according to His promise, you can begin the process of drawing out that gift and letting it shine in your life. Ask yourself, *When is it that I feel God's pleasure the most? What feedback have I gotten from others as I worked in different types of ministries? When do I really feel "on fire" for the Lord?* These are some of the questions that can help you recognize your gift. But if that doesn't work, there is one surefire way to find your gift. Simply listen to God's voice inside your heart. And when you hear Him ask you to do something—do it. You may find that you are operating in your giftedness before you even realize what it is.

CONSIDER THIS!

In a study by the Gallup Organization, the top U.S. city on the "hostility" index is Philadelphia. This index was based on a nine-question survey that asked people how they felt about such things as loud rock music, supermarket checkout lines, and traffic jams. Other cities in the hostility top five were New York, Cleveland, Chicago, and Detroit. At the bottom of the index were Des Moines, Minneapolis, Denver, Seattle, and Honolulu.

Medical experts reviewing the results felt it was no coincidence that the cities ranking high on the hostility index also have higher death rates. Commenting on the study, Dr. Redford Williams of Duke University Medical School said, "Anger kills. There is a strong correlation between hostility and death rates. The angrier people are and the more cynical they are, the shorter their life span."

Do you want to live longer? Then deal with your anger before it deals with you!

KEEP ANGER
IN ITS PLACE

Susan was deeply disappointed at the lack of emotional closeness she felt in her marriage. She began to lash out at her husband. He, of course, reacted with his own defensive anger. Over time their anger grew, threats were exchanged, and eventually divorce became part of their confrontations. Finally, Susan's husband moved out, and she filed for divorce.

IT ISN'T HARD TO MAKE A MOUNTAIN OUT OF A MOLEHILL. JUST ADD A LITTLE DIRT.

The divorce proceedings were bitter. They fought all the way through it. When they met to sign the final papers, they stopped to look at each other, and Susan saw in his eyes the very feelings she was experiencing—a feeling of longing and yet of resignation. She thought, *I don't want to divorce him, and I don't think he wants to divorce me.*

She voiced her thoughts to her husband, and for a moment it appeared he might also soften and admit he, too, still cared. But then he said in a dull monotone, "We've come this far, I guess we should finish it." Susan left the courtroom realizing she had never really wanted a divorce. She just wanted her husband to listen.

Don't allow anger to lead you anywhere, but especially down a road you truly don't want to travel.

Starting a quarrel is like breaching a dam; so drop the matter before a dispute breaks out.

PROVERBS 17:14 NIV

COUNT YOUR BLESSINGS

SOMETIMES WE ARE SO BUSY ADDING UP OUR TROUBLES THAT WE FORGET TO COUNT OUR BLESSINGS.

IN SOME PARTS of Mexico, hot springs and cold springs are found side by side. Because of this natural phenomenon, local women have the convenience of boiling their clothes in the hot springs, then rinsing them in the adjacent cold springs. While watching this procedure a number of years ago, a tourist said to her guide, "I imagine that they think old Mother Nature is pretty generous to supply such ample, clean hot and cold water here side by side for their free use."

The guide replied, "Well, actually, no. There is much grumbling because Mother Nature supplies no soap! And not only that, but the rumor has started to filter in that there are machines that do this work in other parts of the world."

So often we compare our lives to others—what they have in contrast to what we don't have and what they are that we aren't. Such comparisons invariably leave us feeling left out, rejected, and cheated. If we aren't careful to put the brakes on such negative emotions, we can become unnecessarily bitter.

Count your blessings today! If you own one, start with a washing machine.

I will call to mind the deeds of the Lord; I will remember your wonders of old.

PSALM 77:11 NRSV

TOP 10 TIPS

Ten Things to Be Grateful For

1. EACH NEW DAY IS A BRAND-NEW START.

2. GOD LOVES YOU AS IF YOU WERE THE ONLY PERSON HE EVER CREATED.

3. ANYTIME YOU WANT TO TALK TO GOD, HE'S GOT THE TIME TO LISTEN.

4. NO MATTER HOW MANY TIMES YOU ASK GOD TO FORGIVE YOU—HE ALWAYS DOES.

5. YOU HAVE THE PROMISE OF LIVING FOR ALL ETERNITY IN HEAVEN.

6. WHENEVER YOU NEED WISDOM FOR TOUGH DECISIONS, THE HOLY SPIRIT IS THERE TO GIVE IT TO YOU.

7. GOD UNDERSTANDS EVERYTHING YOU'RE GOING THROUGH BETTER THAN ANYONE ELSE EVER COULD.

8. GOD GAVE YOU SPECIAL TALENTS TO DO AMAZING THINGS IN HIS NAME.

9. EACH DAY, GOD IS MOLDING YOU INTO THE IMAGE OF HIS SON.

10. JESUS LOVES YOU SO MUCH THAT HE GAVE UP HIS VERY LIFE FOR YOU!

WATCH YOUR TONGUE!

Laura Ingalls Wilder writes in *Little House in the Ozarks:* "I know a little band of friends that calls itself a woman's club. The avowed purpose of this club is study, but there is an undercurrent of deeper, truer things than even culture and self-improvement. There is no obligation, and there are no promises; but in forming the club and in selecting new members, only those are chosen who are kind-hearted and dependable as well as the possessors of a certain degree of intelligence and a small amount of the genius which is the capacity for careful work. In short, those who are taken into membership are those who will make good friends, and so they are a little band who are each for all and all for each. . . .

> **Whoever** gossips to you will be a gossip of you.

"They are getting so in the habit of speaking good words that I expect to see them all develop into Golden Gossips.

"Ever hear of golden gossip? I read of it some years ago. A woman who was always talking about her friends and neighbors made it her business to talk of them, in fact, but she never said anything but good of them. She was a gossip, but it was 'golden gossip.' This women's club seems to be working in the same way."[28]

Who wouldn't enjoy belonging to such a club?

A gossip goes about telling secrets, but one who is trustworthy in spirit keeps a confidence.

PROVERBS 11:13 NRSV

to do | urgent

#1   There are three essential questions to ask yourself when you talk about others: Is it true? Is it kind? Is it necessary? Make a point during the course of a day to consider each of these questions when you enter into a conversation about another person.

#2   At the end of the day, replay your conversations. Did you violate any of the guidelines? If so, ask for God's forgiveness. Also consider if there's anyone you need to apologize to for saying hurtful things. Finally, ask God to help you to always keep the guidelines in mind so that you can keep your conversation honoring to Him and to others.

"God can heal a broken HEART, but He has to have all the pieces."

ANONYMOUS

GOD'S BEAUTIFUL DESIGN

So many things of beauty begin as "bits and pieces"—not unlike our lives, which often seem like jigsaw puzzles with a multitude of scattered pieces.

Or the artist's collage.

Or a stained glass window.

Or a mosaic floor.

Tragedies and pain can strike any person, and we need to allow the Master Craftsman to put us back together according to His design, rather than trying to find all the pieces and glue ourselves together without Him.

In *The Dark Night of the Soul,* Georgia Harkness writes, "The Christian faith imparts meaning to life. A living faith that is centered in God as revealed in Christ takes our chaotic, disorganized selves, with their crude jumble of pleasures and pains, and knits them together into a steadiness and joy that can endure anything with God."[29]

Trust God today to turn your brokenness into something of beauty and value.

Who's Who:

Lance Armstrong

In July 2004, Lance Armstrong won the Tour de France, the most prestigious race in cycling—for the sixth time in a row! In 1999, the first year Armstrong won, he received a lot of publicity about the fact that he had overcome testicular cancer. But there were those who criticized his win, saying that it happened only because the best competitors were kept out of the race due to a doping scandal. But the next year, when all the best cyclists returned to the race, Armstrong won again.

In analyzing Armstrong's second victory, one commentator mentioned that it was only after the athlete's bout with cancer that he became a world-class cyclist. That's because after his recovery, he weighed 40 pounds less than he did before his illness. And although he added some weight during the subsequent years, he always remained lighter, giving him a winning edge.

The next time adversity comes your way, you can be sure that God will find a way to use it to propel you to a future victory.

Fun Trivia

At one time, people thought that all emotions—whether fear, love, hate, or happiness—all originated in the heart. Later, they believed the only emotion of the heart was love. That's why the heart symbol became the symbol of love.

Look inside your heart today. Is there someone you haven't expressed your love to in a while? Thank God for that person's presence in your heart, then think of a creative way to show him or her just how much you care.

LOVE IN ACTION

Real **friends** are those who,
when you've made a **fool**
of yourself, don't feel you've
done a **permanent** job.

Napoleon went to school in Brienne with a young man named Demasis who greatly admired him. After Napoleon quelled the mob in Paris and served at Toulon, his authority was stripped from him, and he became penniless. We rarely think of Napoleon as struggling through hard times. However, with thoughts of suicide, he proceeded toward a bridge to throw himself into the waters below. On the way he met his old friend Demasis, who asked him what was troubling him.

Napoleon told him bluntly he was without money, his mother was in need, and he despaired of his situation ever changing. "Oh, if that is all," Demasis said, "take this; it will supply your wants." He put a pouch of gold into his hands and walked away. Normally Napoleon would have never taken such a handout, but that night he did, and his hope was renewed.

When Napoleon came to power, he sought far and wide to thank and promote his friend, but he never found him. It was rumored that Demasis lived and served in one of Napoleon's own armies, but never revealed his true identity; rather, he was content to serve quietly in support of the leader he admired.

Sometimes our simple words or deeds make all the difference in the world to someone who doesn't know where to turn.

Love . . . bears all things, believes all things,
hopes all things, endures all
things. Love never fails.

1 CORINTHIANS 13:4,7,8 NKJV

THE PURPOSE-FILLED LIFE

There was a wealthy noblewoman who had grown tired of life. She had everything one could wish for except happiness and contentment. She said, "I am weary of life. I will go to the river and there end my life."

As she walked along, she felt a little hand tugging at her skirts. Looking down, she saw a frail, hungry-looking little boy who pleaded, "There are six of us. We are dying for want of food!" The noblewoman thought, *Why should I not relieve this wretched family? I have the means, and it seems I will have no more use for riches when I am gone.*

Following the little boy, she entered a scene of misery, sick-

> HE WHO IS WAITING FOR SOMETHING TO TURN UP MIGHT START WITH HIS OWN SHIRTSLEEVES.

ness, and want. She opened her purse and emptied its contents. The family members were beside themselves with joy and gratitude. Even more taken with their need, the noblewoman said, "I'll return tomorrow, and I will share with you more of the good things which God has given to me in abundance!"

She left that scene of want and wretchedness rejoicing that the child had found her. For the first time in her life she understood the reason for her wealth. Never again did she think of ending her life, which was now filled with meaning and purpose.

DON'T BE MISLED: NO ONE MAKES A FOOL OF GOD. WHAT A PERSON PLANTS, HE WILL HARVEST.

GALATIANS 6:7 MSG

WISE WORDS

I give you my hands, to do your work.
I give you my feet, to go your way.
I give you my eyes, to see as you do.
I give you my tongue, to speak your words.
I give you my mind, that you may think in me.
I give you my spirit, that you may pray in me.
Above all, I give you my heart,
that you may love in me your Father
and all mankind.
I give you my whole self, that you may grow in me.
So that it is you, Lord Jesus,
Who lives and works and prays in me.

THE GRAIL SOCIETY

booklist

read more about it...manners

These books will help you polish up your manners and put you at the top of everyone's guest list.

- *Social Skills Survival Guide*
  by June Hines Moore

- *Emily Post's Etiquette*
  by Peggy Post

- *The Amy Vanderbilt Complete Book of Etiquette (Updated)*
  by Nancy Tuckerman

- *Letitia Baldridge's New Manners for New Times*
  by Letitia Baldridge

- *Martine's Handbook of Etiquette & Guide to True Politeness*
  by Arthur Martine

GOOD MANNERS COUNT

IT HAS BEEN SAID THAT fish and house guests have one thing in common—after three days they both begin to stink. Depending on the circumstances, a stay may not require that much time before it "goes bad." Generally speaking, the more displaced your hostess has made herself on your account, the shorter your stay should be. Be certain before you visit with relatives or friends that you both know when you will arrive and when you will depart. The old entertainer's rule of thumb, "Leave them wanting more," is good advice for a houseguest.

The same goes for shorter visits—better to leave earlier than later. When the hostess begins to yawn or gather up the dishes, take the hint!

The art of being a good guest is knowing when to leave.

George Washington visited the home of friends one evening, and when the hour came for him to leave, he said good-bye to the adults, then paused at the entrance where a little girl opened the door to let him out. Washington bowed to her and said, "I am sorry, my little dear, to give you so much trouble."

She replied, "I wish, sir, it was to let you in." Now that's a welcome guest!

When you **find** a friend, don't **outwear** your **welcome;** show up at all hours and he'll soon get fed up.

PROVERBS 25:17 MSG

HOW Do YOU MEASURE Up?

The Christian life is a daily commitment to deny ourselves, take up the cross, and follow Him. How does your commitment measure up? Take this quiz to find out.

1. When the alarm goes off in the morning, I:
   A. Press the snooze button and go back to sleep.
   B. Stumble to the kitchen to make coffee.
   C. Spend time committing my day to the Lord.

2. When my Bible study group conflicts with a TV special I've been dying to see, I:
   A. Make up an excuse to stay home.
   B. Invite the group to my house to watch the TV special.
   C. Keep my commitment to attend the study.

3. When I start to lose interest in my personal devotions, I:
   A. Give up on them.
   B. Rationalize that I spend enough time in church and don't really need a personal devotion time too.
   C. Ask God to renew my zeal for spending one-on-one time with Him.

God is completely faithful. He keeps all of His promises—not just a few. He wants you to keep your commitments as well.

A LIFE WELL SPENT

> **IT'S THE LITTLE THINGS IN LIFE THAT DETERMINE THE BIG THINGS.**

In speaking to a group of ministers, Fred Craddock noted the importance of being faithful in the little things of life. He said: "To give my life for Christ appears glorious. To pour myself out for others . . . to pay the ultimate price of martyrdom—I'll do it. I'm ready, Lord, to go out in a blaze of glory.

"We think giving our all to the Lord is like taking a $1,000 bill and laying it on the table—'Here's my life, Lord. I'm giving it all.'

"But the reality for most of us is that He sends us to the bank and has us cash in the $1,000 for quarters. We go through life putting out twenty-five cents here and fifty cents there. Listen to the neighbor kid's troubles instead of saying, 'Get lost.' Go to a committee meeting. Give a cup of water to a shaky old man in a nursing home.

"Usually giving our life to Christ isn't glorious. It's done in all those little acts of love, twenty-five cents at a time. It would be easy to go out in a flash of glory; it's harder to live the Christian life little by little over the long haul."[30]

Ask the Lord to show you how you can spend your life well.

"His lord said to him, 'Well done, good and faithful servant; you were faithful over a few things, I will make you ruler over many things.'"

MATTHEW 25:21 NKJV

THE KINDNESS FACTOR

MILLIE WAS A MENTALLY handicapped adult who lived with her mother in a small town. She was known for her proverbial "green thumb" as a gardener. Lawns, hedges, and flower beds flourished under her loving attention. Millie also volunteered by cutting grass and weeds, raking leaves, and planting flowers in vacant lots throughout the town. She was also known for her oil can. She always carried a small can of lubricating oil in her hip pocket and applied a dose of oil to any squeaky door, hinge, or gate she encountered.

On Sundays Millie went to church with her mother. When teased, she refused to respond in any way other than with good humor and unflappable cheer.

When Millie died, everyone in town showed up for her funeral. There were scores who traveled from distant places to attend, including many of those who had once teased her.

Without consciously attempting to do so, Millie exemplified good citizenship. She worked hard, was an optimist, eased tensions, and was a faithful church member.

Others really do notice the small things we do for them in love and kindness.

> **Forget** yourself for others, and others will not forget you!

Jesus said, "Here is a simple, rule-of-thumb guide for behavior: Ask yourself what you want people to do for you, then grab the initiative and do it for them."

MATTHEW 7:12 MSG

Q I really want to show love and kindness to others, and I know this is what God wants me to do. But my problem is that I don't have much money or time. With those limitations, how am I supposed to obey God's command?

You don't need a lot of money or time to share God's love and kindness with others. In fact, if you are watching and listening, you will find that a number of opportunities will present themselves every day. The trouble is that you may be—as many Christians are—too focused on your own activities and needs to see them.

Just look for "everyday ways" to shine a little heavenly light into another's life. These can be so simple: holding the door for someone, sharing a compliment and sunny smile, extending sincere gratitude for a routine service—these are little things, but they can mean a lot to the recipient. And you'll find that in giving to others, you will receive a wonderful gift in return: the privilege of being like Jesus and bringing glory to His name.

IN SERVICE TO OTHERS

Once, a young orphan girl, despondent and lonely, walked through a meadow and saw a small butterfly caught in a thorn bush. The more the butterfly struggled to free itself, the deeper the thorns cut into its fragile body.

Filled with compassion, the girl released the butterfly. But, instead of flying away, the butterfly transformed into an angel and said gently, "To reward you for your kindness, I will do whatever you would like."

Meet a need; do a good deed!

The girl thought for a moment, then replied, "I want to be happy!"

"Very well," the angel said. Then the heavenly creature leaned close to the girl and whispered something in her ear.

Many years later, as the orphan lay on her deathbed after a full and happy life, her friends gathered around her. "Won't you tell us your secret now," they pleaded. With a labored smile, the woman answered, "An angel told me that no matter where I went in life, I would find people who needed me—people rich or poor, young or old, meek or self-assured—and meeting those needs would bring me happiness and satisfaction."

Somewhere in your life there is someone who needs you. Are you willing to be an angel and meet that need?

Be **devoted** to one **another** in brotherly **love**. **Honor** one **another** above **yourselves**.

ROMANS 12:10 NIV

☑ JUST DO IT

#1   Somehow it seems easier to serve when we know others will notice, but what about when they won't? Choose someone whom you can be a "Secret Saint" to. Once a week for a month, perform a service for that person, and try to do it in secret.

For example, you can send an encouraging, anonymous card or leave a basket of goodies on their front porch. Don't tell anyone what you're doing—and see how good it feels to serve someone, receiving credit for your service from God alone.

"*L*aughter is a **TRANQUILIZER** with no side effects."

MERCELINE COX

PRESCRIPTION: LAUGHTER

Norman Cousins was once asked by a group of physicians to meet with cancer patients at a veterans' hospital. He told how he had lost a quarter in a pay phone. "Operator," he said, "I put in a quarter and didn't get my number." She said, "Sir, if you give me your name and address, we'll mail the coin to you."

He recited a full and long litany of all the steps and procedures and expense involved in returning his coin that way and concluded, "Now, operator, why don't you just return my coin, and let's be friends?"

She repeated her offer and then asked if he had pushed the coin-return plunger. He hadn't, but when he did, the phone box spewed out close to four dollars' worth of change!

The operator said, "Sir, will you please put the coins back in the box?" Cousins replied, "If you give me your name and address, I will be glad to mail you the coins."

The veterans exploded with cheers as Cousins told his story. Then one of the physicians asked, "How many of you came into this room in pain?" More than half raised their hands. "How many of you in the past few minutes had less or no pain?" All nodded "yes."

Laughter—it's one of the best pain medications ever!

Who's Who:

Norman Cousins

In the 1960s, well-known editor Norman Cousins had a serious disease, and doctors predicted that he had only a one in five hundred chance of surviving. But Cousins did beat the odds by rejecting hospital treatment and formulating his own cure. He took large doses of vitamin C, watched Marx Brothers films and Candid Camera reruns, and read only humor books. He found that laughter staved off negativity and depression and helped to relieve his pain. In fact, he discovered that ten minutes of "genuine belly laughter" gave him at least two hours of pain-free sleep. Clearly, laughter is good medicine!

If you are suffering—mentally, physically, emotionally—try the formula that worked for Norman Cousins and is prescribed by Solomon, the wisest man who ever lived. Don't wait for laughter to come knocking; pursue it with a passion. Watch it, read it, sit around and crack jokes with your family and friends. Look for humor in every situation. It's usually there lurking just below the surface. Embrace it as you would a friend and let God's healing balm reach out to you through it.

OUR IMMEASURABLE GOD

Cardinal von Faulhaber of Munich is reported once to have had a conversation with the famed physicist Albert Einstein.

"Cardinal von Faulhaber," Einstein said, "I respect religion, but I believe in mathematics. Probably it is the other way around with you."

"You are mistaken," replied the Cardinal. "To me, both are merely different expressions of the same divine exactness."

"But, your Eminence, what would you say if mathematical science should someday come to conclusions directly contradictory to religious beliefs?"

"Oh," the Cardinal answered with ease, "I have the highest respect for the competence of mathematicians. I am sure they would never rest until they discovered their mistake."

Regardless of how ardently some people try to suppress it, God's truth will always prevail.

GOD PLUS ONE IS ALWAYS A MAJORITY!

IF GOD BE FOR US, WHO CAN BE AGAINST US?

ROMANS 8:31 KJV

WISE WORDS

To say that God is infinite is to say that he is measureless. Measurement is the way created things have of accounting for themselves. It describes limitations, imperfections, and cannot apply to God. Weight describes the gravitational pull of the earth upon material bodies; distance describes intervals between bodies in space; length means extension in space; and there are other familiar measurements such as those for liquid, energy, sound, light, and numbers for pluralities. We also try to measure abstract qualities, and speak of great or little faith, high or low intelligence, large or meager talents. Is it not plain that all this does not and cannot apply to God? . . . He is above all this, outside of it, beyond it.

A. W. TOZER

TO MAKE A FRIEND, BE ONE

YOU CAN WIN MORE FRIENDS WITH YOUR EARS THAN WITH YOUR MOUTH.

DALE CARNEGIE, author of *How To Win Friends and Influence People,* is considered one of the greatest "friend winners" of the century. He taught, "You can make more friends in two months by becoming interested in other people than you can in two years by trying to get other people interested in you."

To illustrate his point, Carnegie would tell how dogs have learned the fine art of making friends better than most people. When you get within ten feet of a friendly dog, he will begin to wag his tail, a visible sign that he welcomes and enjoys your presence. If you take time to pet the dog, he will become excited, lick you, and jump all over you to show how much he appreciates you. The dog became man's best friend by being genuinely interested in people!

One of the foremost ways, of course, in which we show our interest in others is to listen to them—to ask questions, to intently listen to their answers, and to ask further questions based upon what they say. The person who feels "heard" is likely to seek out his friendly listener again and again, and to count that person as a great friend.

Need a friend? Start listening with your heart.

Post this at all the intersections, dear friends: Lead with your ears, follow up with your tongue.

JAMES 1:19 MSG

TOP 10 LIST

Wise Sayings
about Friendship

1. THE WORLD IS ROUND SO THAT FRIENDSHIP MAY ENCIRCLE IT.

2. FRIENDSHIP IS NOT SOMETHING TO GET—
IT IS SOMETHING TO GIVE.

3. THE BANK OF FRIENDSHIP
NEEDS REGULAR DEPOSITS.

4. FRIENDSHIPS WILL LAST IF THEY ARE PUT FIRST.

5. FRIENDSHIP IS THE ONLY CEMENT THAT
WILL HOLD THE WORLD TOGETHER.

6. THE DOOR OF FRIENDSHIP OPENS WIDE WHEN
YOU CLOSE YOUR EYES TO OTHERS' FAULTS.

7. THE BEST RULE OF FRIENDSHIP: KEEP
YOUR HEART SOFTER THAN YOUR HEAD.

8. GOSSIP IS A TORPEDO THAT WILL SINK A FRIENDSHIP.

9. WHERE KINDNESS IS PLANTED,
FRIENDSHIP GROWS.

10. WE ARE NEVER SO RICH THAT WE CAN AFFORD TO LOSE OUR FRIENDSHIPS.

NEVER-ENDING JOY

THE STORY OF HELEN Keller is well-known. Though Helen was deaf and blind from a childhood disease, her teacher, Anne Sullivan, opened the world to her through the other senses of taste, touch, and smell. In her autobiography, Helen Keller wrote:

"Fate—silent, pitiless—bars the way. Fain would I question his imperious decree; for my heart is undisciplined and passionate, but my tongue will not utter the bitter, futile words that rise to my lips, and they fall back into my heart like unshed tears. Silence sits immense upon my soul. Then comes hope with a smile and whispers, 'There is joy in self-forgetfulness.' So I try to make the light in other people's eyes my sun, the music in others' ears my symphony, the smile on others' lips my happiness."

How sad it is when we search only within ourselves for a reason to be happy, because the happiness in those around us is reason enough to have joy, regardless of our situation or handicap. And, if the poor and the handicapped can have joy, how can we wallow in depression?

If we look to Jesus, all will be well with us—inside and out.

lighter up

A woman had just had her annual physical exam and was waiting for the doctor's report. After a few minutes, the doctor came in, charts in hand, and said, "There's no reason why you can't live a completely normal life as long as you don't try to enjoy it."

Do you go through life as if worry and depression were "normal"? Remember, God is the author of joy, and He has an abundance to give you, every minute of every day!

Looking unto Jesus the author

"It's not the **outlook** but the **up-look** that counts."

and finisher of our faith. HEBREWS 12:2 KJV

CONSIDER
THIS!

Consider these acrostics for faith:

Feeling	**F**aith
Afraid	**A**sks
I	**I**mpossible
Trust	**T**hings
Him	**H**umbly

Forsaking	**F**louting
All	**A**ppearances
I	**I**
Take	**T**rust
Him	**H**im

WALKING BY FAITH
NOT SIGHT

Sometimes I'm sad. I know not why
My heart is sore and distressed;
It seems the burdens of this world
Have settled on my heart.
And yet I know . . . I know that God
Who doeth all things right
Will lead me thus to understand
To walk by FAITH . . . not SIGHT.
And though I may not see the way
He's planned for me to go . . .
That way seems dark to me just now
But oh, I'm sure He knows!
Today He guides my feeble step
Tomorrow's in His right . . .
He has asked me to never fear . . .
But walk by FAITH . . . not SIGHT.
Some day the mists will roll away,
The sun will shine again.
I'll see the beauty in the flowers
I'll hear the bird's refrain.
And then I'll know my Father's hand
Has led the way to light
Because I placed my hands in His
And walked by FAITH . . . not SIGHT.
—Ruth A. Morgan[31]

> **Faith is** daring the soul to go beyond what the eyes see.

We walk by faith, not by sight.

2 CORINTHIANS 5:7 KJV

Fun Trivia

How much do you know about sleep?
The following facts and statistics may surprise you!

- Before Thomas Edison invented the light bulb, people slept an average of 10 hours a night.

- Today, Americans average 6.9 hours of sleep on weeknights and 7.5 hours per night on weekends.

- Approximately 70 million Americans are affected by a sleep problem.

- Narcolepsy, a neurological disorder that causes sudden "sleep attacks," affects approximately 293,000 people in the United States.

- According to a recent poll, 51 percent of Americans said they drove while feeling drowsy in the past year; 17 percent said they actually dozed off behind the wheel!

GET YOUR VITAMIN Zs

The best **bridge** between **hope** and **despair** is often a **good** night's **sleep.**

Medical researchers are coming to what may seem to be a common sense conclusion: a missing ingredient to health may be "vitamin Zzzzzzz."

When participants in one study were cheated out of four hours of sleep for four consecutive nights, they had on average a 30 percent drop in their immune systems, as measured by natural killer-cell activity. Such a drop can readily increase a person's susceptibility to colds and flu, and perhaps to other serious diseases. Says sleep researcher Michael Irwin, M.D., "Many people just need a regular-length sleep to get those natural killer cells revved up again."

While a steady diet of sufficient sleep may not completely prevent disease, it can improve the body's defense system and help a person combat disease more efficiently and effectively.

Sleep is the cheapest health aid a person can take. Sleep is God's own means of restoring health to the body, as well as providing rest to the mind. Many have reported a new outlook or a change of heart after a good night's sleep.

Ask God to renew your strength as you sleep tonight, then get to bed on time so He can give you what you requested.

It is vain for you to rise up early, to sit up late, to eat the bread of sorrows; for so He gives His beloved sleep.

PSALM 127:2 KJV

LEARNING TO BE CONTENT

In *Little Women,* Mrs. March tells this story to her daughters:

"Once upon a time, there were four girls who had enough to eat and drink and wear, a good many comforts and pleasures, kind friends and parents—and yet they were not content, always wishing for something more. Finally they asked an old woman for advice. 'When you feel discontented,' she told them, 'think over your blessings, and be grateful.'

> **Be content**
> with what
> you have.
>
> HEBREWS 13:5 NIV

"They decided to try her advice and were surprised to see how well off they were. One girl discovered money couldn't keep shame and sorrow out of rich people's houses. Another learned she was a great deal happier with her youth, health, and good spirits than a certain fretful, feeble old lady who couldn't enjoy her comforts. The third found that, disagreeable as it was to help get dinner, it was harder still to have to go begging for it. The fourth girl learned that even carnelian rings were not so valuable as good behavior. So they agreed to stop complaining and to enjoy the blessings they already possessed."

Wanting something does not mean it's best for us. If you want to be content, learn to be grateful for what you have.

The best way to make
workers miserable is to satisfy
all of their demands.

#1   So often our discontent comes from focusing on what we don't have rather than focusing on, or taking the time to enjoy, what we have. The best cure for the "desire to acquire" is to remove yourself from the temptations. Don't go to the mall "just to look around." Don't go to a bookstore "just to browse." Do your browsing at the library instead.

#2

       The next step is to truly be aware of, and learn to appreciate, what you already have. Go through your clothes carefully. Mend and press the things that need attention. Set aside the items that no longer fit you and give them to a charity. Chances are you'll find clothing you forgot you had that you can enjoy again. The same is true for books! Browse your own bookshelves for a book you haven't read yet—or a favorite you'd like to read again.

#3

#4

#5

#6

#7

#8

#9

#10

"To earn honor is **BETTER** than earning honors."

ANONYMOUS

THE VALUE OF HONOR

Tension hung in the air. Rosalie Elliott had spelled her way to the fourth round of a national spelling bee in Washington, D.C. The eleven-year-old from South Carolina now faced the task of spelling the word "avowal." In her soft southern drawl, she began to recite the letters.

However, when she reached the next to last letter, the judges couldn't discern whether she said "a" or "e." They debated among themselves for several minutes, listening to a tape of Rosalie's effort. The crucial letter, though, was simply too accent-distorted to decipher. Finally, the lead judge sought input from the only person who could provide the answer.

"Was that second to last letter an 'a' or an 'e'?" he asked Rosalie. By this time, thanks to the whispering of her nearby competitors, Rosalie knew the correct spelling. Still, without hesitating, she replied that she had misspelled the word and walked from the stage.

The entire audience—including some fifty newspaper reporters—stood and applauded. The moment was especially proud for her parents. Out of defeat, Rosalie had emerged a victor. And much more was written about her than the child who ultimately won the spelling bee.

Being a person of truth, even when the truth hurts, brings the greatest and most lasting rewards.

Who's Who:

George Washington

George Washington, the first President of the United States of America, is said to have exhibited an honest character even as a small child. When his father asked him who chopped down the cherry tree, he reportedly responded, "I cannot tell a lie. I did it."

The honest boy became the honest man. In later life George Washington was quoted as saying, "I hope I shall always possess firmness and virtue enough to maintain what I consider the most enviable of all titles, the character of an Honest Man." That he is still so highly regarded today is at least in part a tribute to the honesty to which he adhered throughout his lifetime.

THE POWER OF ENCOURAGEMENT

A heart doctor was amazed at the great improvement one of his patients had made. When he had seen the woman a few months earlier, she was seriously ill in the hospital, needing an oxygen mask. He asked the woman what had happened.

The woman said, "I was sure the end was near and that you and your staff had given up hope. However, Thursday morning when you entered with your troops, something happened that changed everything. You listened to my heart; you seemed pleased by the finding, and you announced to all those standing about my bed that I had a 'wholesome gallop.' I knew that the

A MINUTE OF THOUGHT IS WORTH MORE THAN AN HOUR OF TALK.

doctors, in talking to me, might try to soften things. But I knew they wouldn't kid each other. So when I overheard you tell your colleagues I had a wholesome gallop, I figured I still had a lot of kick to my heart and could not be dying. My spirits were for the first time lifted, and I knew I would live and recover."

The heart doctor never told the woman that a third-sound gallop is a poor sign that denotes the heart muscle is straining and usually failing!

Just a few words can be enough to make a difference in a person's life. How important it is to choose our words wisely!

SET A WATCH, O LORD, BEFORE MY MOUTH; KEEP THE DOOR OF MY LIPS.

PSALM 141:3 KJV

WISE WORDS

Discouraged people
don't need critics.
They hurt enough al-
ready. They don't need
more guilt or piled-on
distress. They need
encouragement. They
need a refuge—
a willing, caring,
available someone.

CHARLES R. SWINDOLL

CONNECTING WITH OTHERS

THE GRIEF-STRICKEN mother sat in a hospital room in stunned silence, tears streaming down her cheeks. She had just lost her only child. She gazed into space as the head nurse asked her, "Did you notice the little boy sitting in the hall just outside?" The woman shook her head no.

The nurse continued. "His mother was brought here by ambulance from their poor one-room apartment. The two of them came to this country only three months ago, because all their family members had been killed in the war. They don't know anyone here.

"That little boy has been sitting outside his mother's room every day for a week in hopes his mother would come out of her coma and speak to him."

By now the woman was listening intently as the nurse continued, "Fifteen minutes ago his mother died. It's my job to tell him that, at age seven, he is all alone in the world—there's nobody who even knows his name." The nurse paused and then asked, "I don't suppose you would tell him for me?" The woman stood, dried her tears, and went out to the boy.

She put her arms around the homeless child. She invited him to come with her to her childless home. In the darkest hour of both their lives, they became lights to each other.

> ## lighten up
>
> A classroom full of first graders was discussing a picture of a family. One little boy in the picture had a different color hair than the other family members. One child suggested that he was adopted, and a little girl said, "I know all about adoptions because I was adopted."
>
> "What does it mean to be adopted?" another child asked.
>
> "It means," said the girl, "that you grew in your mommy's heart instead of in her tummy."
>
> The beautiful thing about adoption is that God fills adoptive parents with the ability to love the adopted child just as unconditionally, just as wholeheartedly, as they would a child born to them. This is the way He loves us as His adopted children!

be given unto you." LUKE 6:38 KJV

HOW Do YOU MEASURE Up?

It's easy to second-guess yourself instead of staying true to what you know is the right choice for you.

1. After I sign up for a Bible study at church, I:
   A. Look to see who else signed up.
   B. Compare my leader to the other leaders.
   C. Trust God will help me get the most out of it.

2. If I'm a mom who chooses to work outside the home, I:
   A. Put down stay-at-home moms in order to build myself up.
   B. Feel guilty and miserable about my decision without doing anything about it.
   C. Feel confident this is the best choice for my family at this time.

3. When I look in the mirror, I:
   A. Immediately focus on the things I wish I could change.
   B. Pledge to stop looking in mirrors.
   C. Thank God for creating me to be exactly who I am.

BE TRUE TO YOURSELF

NOBODY CAN MAKE YOU FEEL IN-FERIOR WITHOUT YOUR CONSENT.

ELEANOR ROOSEVELT

Three women on a hike came upon an unlocked cabin deep in the woods. Receiving no response to their knocks, they went inside to find one room, simply furnished. Nothing seemed unusual except that the large, potbellied, cast iron stove was hung from the ceiling, suspended in midair by wires.

The psychologist said, "It is obvious this lonely trapper has elevated his stove so he can curl up under it and experience a return to the womb." The engineer responded, "Nonsense! This is thermodynamics! He has found a way to distribute heat more evenly in his cabin." The theologian interrupted, "I'm sure this has religious meaning. Fire 'lifted up' has been a religious symbol for millennia."

As the three debated, the cabin owner returned. The hikers immediately asked him why the stove was hung by wires from the ceiling. He replied succinctly, "I had plenty of wire, but not much stove pipe."

Others may try to second-guess your motives, downplay your ideas, or insult you, but only you know why you do what you do, what you think and feel, and how you relate to God.

Stay true to who you are in Christ Jesus!

I am fearfully and wonderfully made.

PSALM 139:14 KJV

NEVER GIVE UP

THE DIFFERENCE BETWEEN GENIUS AND STUPIDITY IS THAT GENIUS HAS ITS LIMITS.

THOMAS EDISON

A PARTIALLY deaf boy trudged into his home one day after school. In his hand, he carried a note. It was a note from school officials, suggesting that his parents remove him from school. According to those wise officials, this boy was "too stupid to learn."

Upon reading the note, the boy's mother vowed, "My son Tom isn't too stupid to learn. I'll teach him myself." And that is exactly what she did.

Many years later when Tom died, many Americans paid tribute to him by turning off their lights for one full minute. This was a fitting tribute, for Tom Edison invented the light bulb— along with motion pictures and the phonograph. In all, he was credited with more than a thousand patents. He also had a gift for powerful, motivating words. You will read several of his quotes in this book.

Neither you nor anyone you work with is beyond learning. No one is beyond discovering new ways to express talent, enthusiasm, creativity, and love. No one is beyond receiving affection and encouragement.

Never give up on yourself, no matter what anyone else says. Stand up for others, and encourage them to stay the course as well. Your Heavenly Father hasn't given up on any of you. And He never will.

We are God's workmanship, created in Christ Jesus to do good works, which God prepared in advance for us to do.

EPHESIANS 2:10 NIV

TOP 10 LIST

People who
Persevered

1. AN EXPERT ONCE SAID OF VINCE LOMBARDI: "HE POSSESSES MINIMAL FOOTBALL KNOWLEDGE AND LACKS MOTIVATION."

2. LOUISA MAY ALCOTT WAS ENCOURAGED BY HER FAMILY TO FIND WORK AS A SERVANT OR SEAMSTRESS.

3. BEETHOVEN'S MUSIC TEACHER CALLED HIM HOPELESS AS A COMPOSER.

4. WALT DISNEY WAS FIRED BY A NEWSPAPER EDITOR FOR LACK OF IDEAS.

5. THOMAS EDISON'S TEACHERS SAID HE WAS TOO STUPID TO LEARN ANYTHING.

6. F. W. WOOLWORTH'S EMPLOYERS SAID HE DIDN'T HAVE ENOUGH SENSE TO WAIT UPON CUSTOMERS.

7. HENRY FORD FAILED AND WENT BROKE FIVE TIMES BEFORE HE FINALLY SUCCEEDED.

8. BABE RUTH, FAMOUS FOR SETTING THE HOME RUN RECORD, ALSO HOLDS THE RECORD FOR STRIKEOUTS.

9. WINSTON CHURCHILL FAILED SIXTH GRADE.

10. ALBERT EINSTEIN DID NOT SPEAK UNTIL HE WAS FOUR YEARS OLD AND DIDN'T READ UNTIL HE WAS SEVEN.

TURNING EVERYTHING OVER TO GOD

AT A CRUCIAL TRANSITION time a Christian woman cried out to the Lord, despairing over the lack of spiritual power and fruitfulness she was experiencing in her life. Suddenly she sensed Jesus standing beside her, asking, "May I have the keys to your life?"

The experience was so realistic, the woman reached into her pocket and took out a ring of keys. "Are all the keys here?" the Lord asked.

"Yes, except the key to one small room in my life."

"If you cannot trust Me in all rooms of your life, I cannot ac-cept any of the keys."

The woman was so overwhelmed at the thought of the Lord moving out of her life altogether, she cried, "Lord, take the keys to all the rooms of my life!"

Many of us have rooms we hope no one will ever see. We intend to clean them out someday, but "someday" never seems to come. When we invite Jesus into these rooms, He will help us clean them. With Him, we have the courage to throw away all the "junk" and fill the rooms with His love and peace and joy.

> **Jesus is** a friend who knows all your faults and still loves you anyway.

God **demonstrates** his own love for us in this: While we were still sinners, Christ died for us.

ROMANS 5:8 NIV

Q

I have a hard time trusting God with every area of my life. Do you have any advice to help me trust Him completely?

The next time you're tempted not to trust God, think of yourself as an athlete in training and God as your coach. Athletes are the perfect example of totally trusting someone in authority. A gymnast, for example, who believes completely in her coach will do whatever he says. If the coach tells her to change her technique on the parallel bars, she will do it even if it feels awkward at first. If the coach tells her she needs to focus more when she is on the balance beam, she will do it. Why? Because she believes with her whole heart that her coach knows what it takes to be a winner.

Likewise, you can trust that God knows what it takes to make you a winner. So the next time you're tempted to hold back in your Christian "training," submit to your "coach" in complete obedience. He wants to make you a winner!

LOVE YOUR ENEMIES

On their way back from a meeting of the Greek Orthodox Archdiocese, Father Demetrios Frangos and Father Germanos Stavropoulos were in a car accident. A young woman high on PCP drove into their car while they waited at a stoplight, and both priests were killed instantly. The woman, a legal secretary with a seven-year-old, had no previous police record, but admitted to having used drugs for ten years. She was charged with murder and several other felonies. The tabloid headlines were especially vicious, referring to her as the "priest killer."

Those who deserve love the least need it the most.

Father Demetrios' son, George, responded with forgiveness, not anger. He offered to help provide the woman with a lawyer and hoped if she was convicted the sentence would be short. He said, "The last thing my father would have wanted was to make an example [of her]. This woman is anguished and troubled to begin with . . . we have to look after the innocent one, the child. It is extremely important that her child be told that we forgive her mother."[32]

George Frangos loved his father and grieved for him, but more important to him than "legal justice" was "divine justice"—that this woman and her little daughter know the love of Jesus Christ.

Jesus said, "I say unto you, Love your enemies; bless them that curse you, do good to them that hate you, and pray for them which despitefully use you."

MATTHEW 5:44 KJV

As you go through each day, do you get angry at the little injustices that people impose on you. Maybe it's the person who dashes through the yellow light at an intersection or the person who cuts in front of you at the coffee shop. Or it could be the person who goes through the express lane with more than ten items.

Make it a point one day to count just how many times you feel your temper flare. Then the next day, resolve to stop your anger toward little violations by saying quick prayers for the people who commit them. For example, for the people who cut you off in traffic, pray that they will arrive at their destination safely.

You'll be amazed at how much your attitude changes—and stress level goes down—as you lift before the Lord in prayer those who have wronged you.

Be kind one to another, **TENDERHEARTED,** forgiving one another, as God in Christ has **forgiven** you.

EPHESIANS 4:32 NRSV

PUT THE PAST BEHIND YOU

A much-loved minister of God once carried a secret burden of long-past sin buried deep in his heart. He had committed the sin many years before during his seminary training. No one knew what he had done, but they did know he had repented. Even so, he had suffered years of remorse over the incident without any sense of God's forgiveness.

A woman in his church deeply loved God and claimed to have visions in which Jesus Christ spoke to her. The minister, skeptical of her claims, asked of her, "The next time you speak to the Lord, would you please ask Him what sin your minister committed while he was in seminary?" The woman agreed.

When she came to the church a few days later the minister asked, "Did He visit you?" She said, "Yes."

"And did you ask Him what sin I committed in seminary?"

"Yes, I asked Him," she replied.

"Well, what did He say?"

"He said, 'I don't remember.'"

Who's Who:

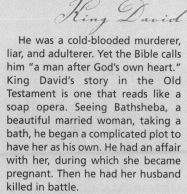

King David

He was a cold-blooded murderer, liar, and adulterer. Yet the Bible calls him "a man after God's own heart." King David's story in the Old Testament is one that reads like a soap opera. Seeing Bathsheba, a beautiful married woman, taking a bath, he began a complicated plot to have her as his own. He had an affair with her, during which she became pregnant. Then he had her husband killed in battle.

It wasn't until the prophet Nathan confronted David with his great sins that the king repented. Several of the chapters in the Book of Psalms are David's heart-rending expressions of deep regret before God. But after repenting, David put his sins behind him and went on to become one of history's greatest kings and men of God.

No matter how great our sins, God is faithful to forgive them when we repent with a sincere heart. He wipes the slate clean and wants us to get beyond our regrets and forge ahead to accomplish great things in His name. Don't get stuck in your regrets. Like King David, put them behind you and move forward with freedom and purpose!

YOUR ATTITUDE CAN SET YOU FREE

A new prison was built in British Columbia to replace the old Fort Alcan prison that had been used to house inmates for hundreds of years. After the prisoners were moved into their new quarters, they became part of a work crew to strip the old prison of lumber, electrical appliances, and plumbing that might be reused. Under the supervision of guards, the inmates began tearing down the old prison walls.

As they did, they were shocked at what they found. Although massive locks had sealed heavy metal doors and two-inch steel bars had covered the windows of the cells, the walls of the prison had actually been made out of paper and clay, painted to resemble iron! If any of the prisoners had given a mighty heave or hard kick against a wall, they might easily have knocked a hole in it, allowing for escape. For years, however, they had huddled in their locked cells, regarding escape as impossible.

Nobody had ever tried to escape because they thought it was impossible.

Many people today are prisoners of fear. They never attempt to pursue their dreams because the thought of reaching them seems impossible. How do you know you can't succeed if you don't try?

> WHETHER YOU THINK YOU CAN OR THINK YOU CAN'T, YOU'RE RIGHT.
>
> HENRY FORD

AS HE THINKETH IN HIS HEART, SO IS HE.

PROVERBS 23:7 KJV

WISE WORDS

Your living is determined not
so much by what life brings
to you as by the attitude you
bring to life; not so much by
what happens to you as by
the way your mind looks at
what happens. Circumstances
and situations do color life,
but you have been given the
mind to choose what the
color shall be.

JOHN HOMER MILLER

CONSIDER
THIS!

Defining Neighbor   LUKE 10:25-37 MSG

A religious scholar stood up with a question to test Jesus, "Teacher, what do I need to do to get eternal life?"

He answered, "What's written in God's Law? How do you interpret it?"

He said, "That you love the Lord your God with all your passion and prayer and muscle and intelligence—and that you love your neighbor as well as you do yourself."

"Good answer!" said Jesus. "Do it, and you'll live."

Looking for a loophole, he asked, "And just how would you define 'neighbor'?"

Jesus answered by telling a story. "There was once a man traveling from Jerusalem to Jericho. On the way he was attacked by robbers. They took his clothes, beat him up, and went off leaving him half-dead. Luckily, a priest was on his way down the same road, but when he saw him he angled across to the other side. Then a Levite religious man showed up; he also avoided the injured man.

"A Samaritan traveling the road came on him. When he saw the man's condition, his heart went out to him. He gave him first aid, disinfecting and bandaging his wounds. Then he lifted him on to his donkey, led him to an inn, and made him comfortable. In the morning he took out two silver coins and gave them to the innkeeper, saying, 'Take good care of him, If it costs any more, put it on my bill—I'll pay you on my way back,'

"What do you think? Which of the three became a neighbor to the man attacked by robbers?"

"The one who treated him kindly," the religious scholar responded.

Jesus said, "Go and do the same."

THE KINDNESS OF STRANGERS

One evening when a woman was driving home, she noticed a truck driving very close behind her. She stepped on the gas to put a little distance between them, but when she sped up, the truck did too. The faster she drove, the faster he drove.

Frightened at being pursued this way, she got off the freeway, but the truck followed her. She turned up a main street, hoping to lose him in traffic, but he even ran a red light in pursuit. Finally, near the point of panic, she pulled into a service station and bolted out of her car screaming for help. She was horrified to see the truck driver spring from his vehicle and run toward her.

But then . . . not even looking at her, he yanked open the back door of her vehicle and pulled out a man who was hiding on the floor of her back seat.

Her pursuer had not been the real potential for danger in her life! The truck driver had spotted the man, a convicted rapist, leaving a café and hiding in her car shortly before she returned. His chase was not an effort to harm her, but to save her, even at the risk of his own life.

We often find true, faithful friends in those who have been close to us for years, but rarely in strangers.

A TRUE FRIEND NEVER GETS IN YOUR WAY UNLESS YOU HAPPEN TO BE GOING DOWN.

ARNOLD H. GLASGOW

A **friend** loves at **all** times, and a **brother** is born for **adversity**.

PROVERBS 17:17 NASB

Ward Kimball, one of the animators for Walt Disney's film *Snow White,* worked 240 days on a four-and-one-half-minute sequence in which the dwarfs made soup for Snow White, almost destroying the kitchen in the process. Disney thought the sequence was good, but he decided that it impeded the overall flow of the film, so he took it out.

When the film of your life is shown, will it be the best it can be? A lot will depend on how many of the "good" things you eliminated to make way for the great things God wanted to do through you.

FOCUSING ON WHAT MATTERS MOST

Our greatest **danger** in life is
in permitting the **urgent** things
to **crowd** out the **important.**

CHARLES E. HUMMELL

A time-management expert addressed a group of business students. He pulled out a one-gallon Mason jar and set it on the table. Then he produced a dozen fist-sized rocks and carefully placed them into the jar. Then he asked, "Is this jar full?"

Everyone said yes. Then he reached under the table and pulled out a bucket of gravel. He dumped it in and shook the jar. He asked the group again, "Is the jar full?"

By this time the class was on to him. "Probably not," one student answered. Then the instructor reached under the table and grabbed a bucket of sand. He dumped the sand, which went into all of the spaces between the rocks and the gravel. He asked, "Is this jar full?"

"No!" the class shouted.

Next, he grabbed a pitcher of water and began to pour it in until the jar was filled to the brim. "What is the point of this illustration?" he asked.

One student offered, "No matter how full your schedule is, you can always fit some more things in it!"

"No," the speaker replied, "the truth this illustration teaches us is: if you don't put the big rocks in first, you'll never get them in."

Ask yourself, "What are the 'big rocks' in my life?" Put those in your jar first.

Jesus said, "Where your treasure
is, there your heart will be also."

MATTHEW 6:21 NIV

SAME PLACE, SAME TIME

> OUR **DAYS** ARE IDENTICAL **SUITCASES**—ALL THE **SAME** SIZE—BUT SOME PEOPLE CAN PACK **MORE** INTO THEM THAN OTHERS.

MARY SMITH went to church one Sunday morning and winced when she heard the organist miss a note during the processional. She noted a teenager talking while everybody was supposed to be in prayer. She also couldn't help but notice that several blooms in the altar bouquets were wilted. She felt the usher was scrutinizing what every person was putting into the offering plate, which made her angry. She counted at least five grammatical errors made by the preacher in his sermon. As she left the church through the side door after the closing hymn, she thought, *What a careless group of people!*

Amy Jones went to church one Sunday morning and was thrilled at the arrangement she heard of "A Mighty Fortress." Her heart was touched at hearing a teenager read the morning Scripture lesson. She was encouraged to see the church take up an offering to help hungry children in Nigeria. The preacher's sermon answered a question that had bothered her for some time. She felt radiant joy from the choir members during the recessional. She left the church thinking, *What a wonderful place to worship God!*

Mary and Amy went to the same church, on the same Sunday morning.

Be very careful, then, how you live—not as unwise but as wise, making the most of every opportunity.

EPHESIANS 5:15-16 NIV

TOP **10** LIST

Ways to Know
You're an Optimist

1. YOU BLAME THE DRY CLEANER FOR YOUR SHRUNKEN WAISTBANDS.

2. YOU PUT YOUR SHOES ON WHEN THE PREACHER SAYS, "NOW IN CONCLUSION . . ."

3. YOU THINK THERE IS REALLY SUCH A THING AS AN UNINTERRUPTED BATH.

4. YOU ACTUALLY BELIEVE THAT NO ONE WILL NOTICE THE RUN IN YOUR PANTY HOSE.

5. YOU BELIEVE THE APPLIANCE REPAIRMAN WHEN HE SAYS YOU'RE THE FIRST APPOINTMENT OF THE DAY.

6. YOU'RE SURE YOU KILLED THE ONLY MOUSE IN THE PANTRY.

7. YOU BELIEVE THE PHONE WON'T RING AT 8 A. M. ON SATURDAY MORNING.

8. YOU BELIEVE YOUR SON WHEN HE SAYS, "CAN'T WE GET A DOG? I PROMISE I'LL TAKE CARE OF IT."

9. YOU'RE SURE YOU DON'T LOOK ANYTHING LIKE YOUR MOTHER.

10. YOU ARE HAPPIER AND HEALTHIER BECAUSE YOU SEE GOD IN YOUR CIRCUMSTANCES AND EXPECT THE BEST FROM OTHERS.

HOW WARS ARE STARTED

A LITTLE GIRL ONCE ASKED her father how wars got started.

"Well," said her father, "suppose America persisted in quarreling with England, and. . . . "

"But," interrupted her mother, "America must never quarrel with England."

"I know," said the father, "but I am only using a hypothetical instance."

"But you are misleading the child," protested Mom.

"No, I am not," replied the father indignantly, with an edge of anger in his tone.

"Never mind, Daddy," the little girl interjected, "I think I know how wars get started."

{ **A critical spirit** is like poison ivy—it takes only a little contact to spread the poison. }

Most major arguments don't begin large, but are rooted in a small annoyance, breach, or trespass. It's like the mighty oak that stood on the skyline of the Rocky Mountains. The tree had survived hail, heavy snows, bitter cold, and ferocious storms for more than a century. It was finally felled not by a great lightning strike or an avalanche, but by an attack of tiny beetles.

A little hurt, neglect, or insult can be the beginning of the end for virtually any relationship. Therefore, take care what you say and be certain the attitude you have is right!

Avoid **worldly** and
empty chatter, for it will **lead**
to further **ungodliness.**

2 TIMOTHY 2:16 NASB

new insights into ageless questions

I don't mean to be critical, but what can I do when I see so many things that are wrong. My husband doesn't pick up after himself, and my children can't or won't obey me. I give them instructions, but no one listens. At work, I have the same challenges. It seems as if no one wants to do things the way they should be done. What can I do to make them see the light?

You are obviously a person who sees the details in life. You probably notice if a book is crooked on the shelf or a child's shoelace is untied. You should see your awareness as a gift that God has given you. Used properly it will serve you and those around you very well. The key phrase there is—used properly. It's important for you to realize that most other people don't see things in the same way you do. Constantly correcting and criticizing won't change that. Instead of seeing the imperfection, the thing to be corrected, they see a cranky mom, wife, or coworker.

It may be time for you to make a few adjustments for the sake of others. If it's just a little thing—let it go. Sure, that's hard, but try to remember that God sees all your imperfections, but He doesn't point them out. He covers them with lovingkindness. He would want you to do the same, and consciously focusing on that will help you turn criticism into kindness.

JUST LAUGH ABOUT IT

ON A HOT JUNE DAY, Winona and Will had just exchanged their wedding vows and were about to take their triumphant wedding march back down the aisle. Suddenly Winona's six-foot-tall brother—a groomsman—fainted, and not very delicately at that. In the course of his falling, he toppled another groomsman and lurched against the best man, nearly forcing him down too. Two attendants each grabbed an arm of the fallen man and dragged him out of the church, in full view of the three hundred guests and a horrified young bride.

Winona had no doubt her wedding was ruined and she would be the laughing-stock of the town. It was all she could do to keep back the tears as she walked down the aisle with Will. As they neared the back of the church, however, Will burst into laughter—a big, booming, infectious laugh—and Winona had to laugh too. Soon the entire church was guffawing with gusto.

Winona said many years later, "My first reaction to nearly any situation used to be 'Oh, no,' but Will's first reaction has always been to see humor in a situation. I've grown to adopt his point of view. I figure the very least I can glean from a nightmare is a good laugh and a memorable story to tell later."[33]

lighter up

All eyes were on the radiant bride as her father escorted her down the aisle. They reached the altar and the waiting bridegroom; the bride kissed her father and placed something in his hand. Those in the front pews responded with ripples of laughter. Even the minister smiled broadly. As her father gave her away in marriage, the bride gave him back his credit card.

A little girl attending her first wedding asked her mother why the bride had changed her mind?"

"Whatever do you mean?" her mother asked.

"Well ... she walked into the wedding with one husband and she walked out with a different one."

Then our mouth was filled with laughter, said among the nations, "The Lord has done

> "Humor is to life what shock absorbers are to automobiles."

and our tongue with singing. Then they great things for them." PSALM 126:2 NKJV

booklist

read more about it...forgiveness

- *Forgiveness Is a Choice: A Step by Step Process for Resolving Anger and Restoring Hope*
  by Robert D. Enright

- *Total Forgiveness*
  by R. T. Kendall

- *Forgiveness: How to Make Peace with Your Past and Get on with Your Life*
  by Susanne Simon; Dr. Sidney B. Simon

TOGETHER AGAIN

MEREDITH WAS SURPRISED to find a letter in her mailbox from her brother, Tim. It had been three years since she had spoken to him, even though they lived in the same town. In the letter, Tim told her he and his wife were expecting twins and he hoped she would come to visit the babies after they were born. He expressed his sorrow that they had not communicated more and apologized for whatever it was he had done to cause them to be estranged.

Meredith's initial reaction was one of anger. "Whatever it was?" Didn't he know? She immediately sat down and wrote a five-page letter detailing all the wrongs Tim had committed that hurt her. The phone rang, however, before she could put her letter in an envelope, and it was several hours before she returned to her writing desk. Upon rereading her letter, she was horrified at what she found.

She had thought she was being very matter of fact, but her words were full of anger and pain. Tears of forgiveness filled her eyes. Perhaps it wasn't all Tim's fault.

She called him the next day to say, "I can hardly wait to be the aunt of twins!"

> **To forgive is** to set a prisoner free and discover the prisoner was you.

Jesus said, "If ye forgive men their trespasses, your heavenly Father will also forgive you: But if ye forgive not men their trespasses, neither will your Father forgive your trespasses."

MATTHEW 6:14-15 KJV

KINDNESS PAYS IN BIG WAYS

A number of years ago, the Advertising and Sales Executive Club sponsored a Courtesy Campaign in Kansas City. One thousand silver dollars were flown in from Denver. Then, over a period of days, "mystery shoppers" visited all types of stores, banks, and other places of business. They listened to telephone operators and observed bus and street-car drivers. Each day they filed a written report on the persons they found to be the most courteous.

> **Kindness** is the oil that takes the friction out of life.

Those chosen as the most courteous people in the city received a silver dollar, along with a "courtesy pays" button and a congratulatory card. The fifteen most outstandingly courteous people were guests at the banquet, where they were awarded $25 each. In all, more than 100 people were honored.

What resulted was not only a temporary increase in the courtesy of the local residents, but an awareness throughout the city that simple kindness is a nice thing with which to live! The "residual effect" remained long after the campaign, to the point where Kansas City is still regarded as one of the friendliest cities in the nation.

It doesn't cost anything to be kind, but kindness can pay off in big ways quite apart from money.

The fruit of the Spirit is . . . kindness.

GALATIANS 5:22 NIV

#1   When you are feeling down, discouraged, disappointed, blue, try this to give you a boost. Sit down at your desk, and make a list of the kindnesses others have done for you or your family members. It may be tough at first. But once you remember one and write it #2   down, you will probably have remembered another.

Someone brought you a hot meal when you were sick. Someone gave you a ride when you ran out of gas. Someone paid you a com- #3   pliment when you were feeling old and unattractive. Someone shared their abundant garden with you. Someone allowed you to go in front of them in line. Someone offered to babysit so you could #4   have some time away. Someone gave you directions that helped you get where you were trying to go. No kindness is too small to add to the list.

Leave the list out on your desk and add to it often. Use it to in- #5   spire you to initiate conscious acts of kindness toward others.

#6

#7

#8

#9

#10

CONSIDER
THIS!

In Matthew 13:44-46, Jesus described to His disciples the great value of the gift God had given them. "God's kingdom is like a treasure hidden in a field for years and then accidentally found by a trespasser. The finder is ecstatic—what a field!—and proceeds to sell everything he owns to raise money and buy that field. Or, God's kingdom is like a jewel merchant on the hunt for excellent pearls. Finding one that is flawless, he immediately sells everything and buys it." (MSG).

How much do you value your relationship with God? Do you treasure it above all your earthly possessions? You should.

THE GREATEST TREASURE

While serving in India, a devout English judge befriended a young Indian man. Having been raised in a prominent Indian family, he had been cast out after he converted to Christianity. The judge took the boy into his household where he happily worked as a houseboy.

It was the custom of the household to have a devotional time every evening. One night the judge read aloud the words of Jesus: "Every one that hath forsaken houses, or brethren, or sisters, or father, or mother, or wife, or children, or lands, for my name's sake, shall receive a hundredfold" (Matthew 19:29).

The judge turned to the lad

JESUS IS A FRIEND WHO WALKS IN WHEN THE WORLD HAS WALKED OUT.

and said, "No one here has done this except you, Norbudur. Will you tell us, is it true what Jesus has said?"

The young Indian man read the verse aloud for himself and then turned to the family and said, "No, there is an error."

Startled the judge responded, "There is?"

The youth replied, "It says He gives a hundredfold. I know He gives a thousandfold."

With eternal life, intimacy with the Father, and all the riches of Heaven, who can truly measure the value of what it means when Jesus Christ comes into a person's life?

Jesus said, "These things I have spoken unto you, that in me ye might have peace. In the world ye shall have tribulation: but be of good cheer; I have overcome the world."

JOHN 16:33 KJV

"The past should be a SPRINGBOARD, not a hammock."

IVERN BALL

> **This one thing I do, forgetting those things which are behind, and reaching forth unto those things which are before.**
>
> PHILIPPIANS 3:13 KJV

FINISHING WELL

Many people are good starters but poor finishers. When the going starts getting tough they listen to the little imp on their shoulder that whispers, "You can't do it" and "You'll never make it." Many others do not even start.

What we must realize is that while "doing something" requires a risk, so does "doing nothing." The risk of action may be failure, but the risks of a failure to act can be stagnation, dissatisfaction, and frustration . . . even loss to an evil enemy.

The story of the covered wagon crossing the plains toward the Golden West began with a song:

The Coward never started;
The Weak died on the way;
Only the Strong came through!

That's the way it is in life. But strength does not refer only to physical strength. True strength flows from the strong spirit—a spirit made powerful by a close relationship with God. He gives us the will to succeed, the dreams that will not die, and the wisdom to turn any evil into a blessing.

Lean on God for direction, and keep leaning on Him for the wisdom and courage to finish what you begin!

Who's Who:

Eric Liddell was a well-known sprinter in his native Scotland, known in part for his unusual style of running with his head back and his knees high. When asked how he could see the finish line in that position, he characteristically replied in his Scottish brogue, "The Lord guides me." Having qualified for the Paris Olympics in 1924, Liddell waited excitedly for the posting of the Olympic heats for his best events: the 100 meters and the 4X100 and 4X400 relays. But when he learned that the preliminary dashes were on Sunday he was shocked. "I'm not running," he simply said, and then began training for the 200-meter and 400-meter dashes.

Liddell wouldn't run because he considered Sunday to be sacred, and he was willing to stick by his beliefs even at the risk of sacrificing fame. When the time came to run the 200-meter sprint, he gave it his all and unexpectedly took the bronze medal! Then he put everything he had into the 400-meter sprint, and when it was all over, "The Flying Scotsman" had a gold medal and a world record—all while holding fast to his convictions and his faith.

Eric Liddell continued to "finish well" as a missionary in China and then as an inspiration to fellow prisoners in a Japanese internment camp where he died of a brain tumor in 1945. No doubt the Lord was pleased to welcome him across the finish line! The acclaimed movie *Chariots of Fire* chronicles his life story.

SOMETHING GOOD

Wouldn't this world be better,
If folks whom we meet would say,
"I know something good about you,"
And treat you just that way?
Wouldn't it be splendid,
If each handshake, good and true,
Carried with it this assurance:
"I know something good about you"?
Wouldn't life be happier,
If the good that's in us all,
Were the only thing about us
That people would recall?
Wouldn't our days be sweeter,
If we praised the good we see?
For there is a lot of goodness,
In the worst of you and me.
Wouldn't it be fine to practice
This way of thinking too;
You know something good about me,
I know something good about you?[34]

> **Two things** are hard on the heart—running upstairs and running down people.

Since we can never know or tell the full story about any other human being, why not just skip to the good highlights?

Let no **corrupt** communication **proceed** out of your mouth, but that which is good to the use of edifying, that it may minister grace unto the hearers.

EPHESIANS 4:29 KJV

new insights into ageless questions

One of my coworkers is always coming into my office and gossiping about the other women in our department. I try not to encourage her or act like I'm interested, but she doesn't seem to get the hint. What can I do?

Acting disinterested and hoping your coworker will get the hint just won't get it. There is only one way to stop gossip—that's to speak up. The less intrusive way is to say something positive about a person your coworker has just shared something negative about. "I heard that Susan is getting a divorce." Follow that by saying: "Susan is a great person. Her business is not our business, but I bet she could really use our prayers right now."

If that doesn't work, you might try another angle. Explain to your coworker that you are making an effort to speak positively about others, and you are having a difficult time. Ask her if she would help you—as a favor—by sharing only positive things with you.

booklist

- *A Guide to Prayer for Ministers and Other Servants*
  by Reuben P. Job; Normal Shawchuck
- *Improving Your Serve*
  by Charles R. Swindoll
- *Serving Lessons*
  by Bill Hybels

WE ARE WHAT WE HAVE RECEIVED

ALBERT EINSTEIN ONCE reflected on the purpose of man's existence: "Strange is our situation here upon earth. Each of us comes for a short visit, not knowing why, yet sometimes seeming to a divine purpose. From the standpoint of daily life, however, there is one thing we do know: That we are here for the sake of others . . . for the countless unknown souls with whose fate we are connected by a bond of sympathy. Many times a day, I realize how much my own outer and inner life is built upon the labors of people, both living and dead, and how earnestly I must exert myself in order to give in return as much as I have received."

When we truly take stock of our lives, we must admit we have done nothing solely on our own. Our thinking has been fashioned by our many teachers and mentors, including family members. Our ability to function physically is the result, in part, of our genetic code and the productivity of others in providing food, water, and shelter. Our spiritual lives are a gift of God himself. We are what we have received.

Our reaction to these facts drives each of us to give to others the good things we have been fortunate to receive. This is what being a citizen of God's kingdom is all about.

> **The heart** is the happiest when it beats for others.

Greater **love** hath no man than this, that a man
lay down his life for his **friends.**

JOHN 15:13 KJV

LEADERS KEEP TRYING

In 1991 Anne Busquet was general manager of the Optima Card division for American Express. When five of her two thousand employees were found to have hidden $24 million in losses, she was held accountable. Busquet had to face the fact that, as an intense perfectionist, she apparently came across as intimidating and confrontational to her subordinates—to the point they were more willing to lie than to report bad news to her!

Busquet lost her Optima job, but was given a second chance by American Express: an opportunity to salvage one of its smaller businesses. Her self-esteem shaken, she nearly turned down the offer. Then she decided this was her chance to alter the way she related to others. She took on the new job as a personal challenge to change.

Realizing she had to be much more understanding, she began to work on being more patient and listening more carefully and intently. She learned to solicit bad news in an unintimidating way.

Four years after she was removed from her previous position, Ann Busquet was promoted to be an executive vice-president at American Express.

Failure is not the end; it is a teacher for a new beginning and a better life.

> FAILURE IS NOT FALLING DOWN. IT'S STAYING DOWN.
> MARY PICKFORD

NO MATTER HOW MANY TIMES YOU TRIP THEM UP, GOD-LOYAL PEOPLE DON'T STAY DOWN LONG; SOON THEY'RE UP ON THEIR FEET.
PROVERBS 24:16 MSG

WISE WORDS

If you have made mistakes, even serious mistakes, there is always another chance for you. And supposing you have tried and failed again and again, you may have a fresh start any moment you choose, for this thing that we call "failure" is not the falling down, but the staying down.

MARY PICKFORD

Fun Trivia

How much do you know about laughter?

- Humans are one of the only species that laugh.
- The average adult laughs seventeen times a day.
- Laughter is actually a complex response that involves many of the same skills used in solving problems.
- There is strong evidence that laughter can improve health and help fight disease.
- Evidence shows that laughter strengthens your immune system.
- Laughter is thought to increase intellectual performance and boost information retention.
- Laughter enhances creativity.
- Laughter encourages teambuilding in the workplace.
- Laughter is a major stress reliever.
- Laughter increases joy and the sense of being alive!

GOD'S GIFT OF LAUGHTER

Laughter is the **brush** that **sweeps** away the **cobwebs** of the **heart.** MORT WALKER

In *Growing Strong in the Seasons of Life,* Charles Swindoll writes: "Tonight was fun 'n' games night around the supper table in our house. It was wild. First of all, one of the kids snickered during the prayer (which isn't that unusual), and that tipped the first domino. Then a humorous incident from school was shared, and the event (as well as how it was told) triggered havoc around the table. That was the beginning of twenty to thirty minutes of the loudest, silliest, most enjoyable laughter you can imagine. At one point I watched my oldest literally fall off his chair in hysterics, my youngest doubled over in his chair as his face wound up in his plate with corn chips stuck to his cheeks . . . and my two girls leaning back, lost and preoccupied in the most beautiful and beneficial therapy God ever granted humanity: laughter.

"What is so amazing is that everything seemed far less serious and heavy. Irritability and impatience were ignored like unwanted guests. For example, during the meal little Chuck spilled his drink twice . . . and even that brought the house down. If I remember correctly, that made six times during the day he accidentally spilled his drink, but nobody bothered to count."[35]

Laughter—what a treasure it is!

A happy heart is good medicine and a cheerful mind works healing, but a broken spirit dries up the bones.

PROVERBS 17:22 AMP

MAKING THE PRESENT COUNT

Psychologist William Marston once asked three thousand people, "What have you to live for?" He was shocked to discover that 94 percent of the people he polled were simply enduring the present while they waited for the future. Some indicated they were waiting for "something" to happen—waiting for children to grow up and leave home, waiting for next year, waiting for another time to take a long-awaited trip, waiting for someone to die, or waiting for tomorrow. They had hope, but no ongoing purpose to their lives!

Only 6 percent of the people identified relationships and activities in the present tense of their lives that they counted as valuable reasons for living!

The 94 percent would be wise to recall the words of this poem by an unknown author:

"During all the years since time began, Today has been the friend of man; But in his blindness and his sorrow, He looks to yesterday and tomorrow. Forget past trials and your sorrow. There was, but is, no yesterday, And there may be no tomorrow."

> **Guilt is** concerned with the past. Worry is concerned about the future. Contentment enjoys the present.

Not that I am implying that I was in any personal want, for I have learned how to be content [satisfied to the point where I am not disturbed or disquieted] in whatever state I am.

PHILIPPIANS 4:11 AMP

#1   Do you have days when you feel bogged down by the past, pessimistic about the future, and unable to deal with the present? Try cleaning out a closet. You will need large trash bags and several boxes. Mark them for throw-away or give-away. The bags are for **#2** clothing and the boxes are for other items.

Begin by taking everything out of the closet. That's right—everything! Wipe down the shelves and hanger racks with a damp cloth. Spray with a nice room freshener. Vacuum the floor. Then **#3** begin to go through the items one at a time. If you want to keep it, find a place for it in the closet. If you choose not to keep it, place it in the appropriate bag or box.

#4   When you're finished, you should have a clean, sweet-smelling closet that will be a present-day pleasure, a good bit of the past to throw away and put behind you forever, and a nice assortment of items that will bless others in the future. Take those to your local **#5** church, charity, or thrift shop.

#6

#7

#8

#9

#10

REFERENCES

ENDNOTES

1. *Little House in the Ozarks*, Laura Ingalls Wilder (Nashville, TN: Thomas Nelson Publishers, 1991), p. 68.

2. "Mottoes," Kalends, *The New Speaker's Treasury of Wit and Wisdom*, Herbert V. Prochnow, ed. (New York, NY: Harper & Row, 1958), p. 290.

3. *Words to Love By*, Mother Teresa (Notre Dame, IN : Ave Maria Press, 1983), pp. 55, 59.

4. *Illustrations for Preaching and Teaching*, Craig Brian Larson, ed. (Grand Rapids, MI: Baker Books, 1993), p. 119.

5. *Especially for a Woman*, Ann Kiemel Anderson (Nashville, TN: Thomas Nelson Publishers, 1994), p. 42.

6. "That's What Friends Are For," by Jane Gross, *Ladies Home Journal*, July 1995, p. 146.

7. Story from *Illustrations Unlimited*, James Hewett, ed. (Wheaton, IL: Tyndale House Publishers, 1988), pp. 131-132.

8. *Little House in the Ozarks*, Laura Ingalls Wilder (Nashville, TN: Thomas Nelson Publishers, 1991), p. 36.

9. *A Closer Walk*, Catherine Marshall (Grand Rapids, MI: Fleming H. Revell, Division of Baker Book House Co., 1986), pp. 87-88.

10. *Illustrations for Preaching and Teaching*, Craig Brian Larson, ed. (Grand Rapids, MI: Baker Books, 1993), p. 97.

11. Ibid., p.187.

12. *Family Circle*, September 1, 1995, p. 114.

13. *It's My Turn*, Ruth Bell Graham (Minneapolis, MN: Grason, 1982), p. 110.

14. *Dakota*, Kathleen Norris, (New York, NY: Houghton Mifflin, 1993), p. 114.

15. *People*, March 20, 1995, pp. 87-88.

16. "A Character Quiz," Herbert V. Prochnow, *The Speaker's Book of Illustrations*, Herbert V. Prochnow, ed. (Grand Rapids, MI: Baker Book House, 1960), p. 100.

17. "Janette Oke: Pioneer Novelist," Nancy McGough, *Homelife*, November 1995, pp. 12, 14-15.

18. *Learning to Forgive*, Doris Donnelly (New York, NY: Macmillan Publishing, 1979), pp. 24-25.

19. *Newsweek*, April 24, 1995, p. 150.

20. "Anatomy of a Champion," George Sheehan, *Runner's World*, May 1993, p. 18.

21. "Signs and Wonders," John Garvey, *Commonweal*, April 22, 1994, p. 10.

22. *A Lamp for My Feet*, Elisabeth Elliot (Ann Arbor, MI: Servant Publications, 1987), p. 52.

23. *Illustrations for Preaching and Teaching*, Craig Brian Larson, ed. (Grand Rapids, MI: Baker Books, 1993).

24. Ibid., p. 200.

25. *Let Me Illustrate*, Albert P. Stauderman (Minneapolis, MN: Augsburg Press, 1983), p. 104.

26. *TV Guide*, July 22 1995, p. 29.

27. *Especially for a Woman*, Beverly LaHaye (Nashville, TN: Thomas Nelson, 1994), pp. 253, 263.

28. *Little House in the Ozarks*, Laura Ingalls Wilder (Nashville, TN: Thomas Nelson Publishers, 1991), p. 103.

29. *The Dark Night of the Soul*, Georgia Harkness (New York, NY: Abingdon Press, 1945).

30. "Of Love and Loss," Jennet Conant, *Redbook*, October 1994, p. 82.

31. "By Faith Not Sight," Ruth A. Morgan, *Encyclopedia of 7700 Illustrations*, Paul Lee Tan, ed. (Rockville, MD: Assurance Publishers, 1979), p. 404.

32. *Decision*, September 1995, pp. 4-5.

33. "Disaster Weddings and How Couples Coped," Barbara Rachel Pollack, *Redbook*, August 1995, p. 102.

34. "I Know Something Good about You," *Knight's Master Book of New Illustrations*, Walter B. Knight (Grand Rapids, MI: Eerdmans Pub. Co., 1956), pp. 174-175.

35. *Growing Strong in the Seasons of Life*, Charles Swindoll (Portland, OR: Multnomah Press, 1983), p. 100.

Additional copies of this book and other
titles from Honor Books
are available from your local bookstore.

These books are also available in this series:

God's Devotional Book
God's Devotional Book for Mothers
God's Devotional Book for Teens

If you have enjoyed this book,
or if it has impacted your life,
we would like to hear from you.
Please contact us at:

Honor Books
An Imprint of Cook Communication Ministries
4050 Lee Vance View
Colorado Springs, CO 80918
www.cookministries.com